Fighting
the
Good Fight
of
Faith

By Lois Kirwan

Fighting the Good Fight of Faith
Published by Leading Through Living Community LLC

Copyright 2018 by Lois Kirwan

ISBN-13: 978-0-9991308-4-1

Scripture quotations are from the Holy Bible, King James Version (KJV) -
www.Bible.com

For information:
Leading Through Living Community LLC
6790 W. Broad Street
Douglasville, GA 30134

DEDICATION & ACKNOWLEDGEMENTS

Ever since I was a child, I enjoyed writing and that passion only got more intense with age. If I had my way and was dealt the right hand, I would have written countless books by now. I always wanted to be a published author and knew that my love for English and English literature would someday pay off.

Amidst all the poems, songs, comedy skits, and other writing, I realized one day that I had always had to fight for whatever I wanted. I decided to put my faith into action and commenced to writing this book, *Fighting the Good Fight of Faith*.

I've been at it for a long time and never thought about actually finishing it. I thought someone needed to discover me first, and then things would go from there... Until one day I was in the kitchen and a gentle yet firm voice said to me, "Lois, you are a writer so just write!"

John 10:27 states, "My sheep hear my voice."

I knew that voice calling me to write was the voice of the Lord, so from that point forward I became a lot more diligent and was determined to see this book through, come what may.

Having said all that, I want to give thanks first and foremost to God the Father, God the Son, and God the

Holy Spirit, without whom I would and could not accomplish what I have so far.

Next, I want to acknowledge and say thank you to one of the most beautiful ladies that I have ever had the privilege of knowing and the honor of calling my friend Mrs. Nikki Welsh. Before I even claimed her as a friend, she went out of her way and incorporated other co-workers to raise funds without my knowledge to make sure that the kids and I had a beautiful and enjoyable time at Disney World in Orlando. Nikki, you have a heart of gold! You help everyone you know has a need and encourage others to help also. You have been my biggest supporter, and when you heard that I was writing this book, you believed in me more than I believed in myself and gave me the confidence to think that I really might be able to do this thing. When I felt low, without even saying anything, you lifted my spirit with your words of encouragement and hope. I love you Nikki and I pray that the favor of God rest on your life and the rest of your family.

Last, but not least, I want to say thanks to my kids who have always been there for me and have helped me with the computer and other technical issues. They have seen firsthand how God always comes through and makes a way out of no way. You guys are my peeps.

TABLE OF CONTENTS

INTRODUCTION

Growing up on the very small island of Montserrat, I could recall from a very early age that I had to trust God for even some basic needs in life such as food and clothing. My mother stayed at home and did the chores, and my father, who was a laborer, worked but did not have a steady job.

There were times when I left for school in the morning that there was no food in the house, and even as I walked home at lunch time, I really did not expect to have lunch. I went home anyway because I figured that I would go through the motions, for whether we had or did not have food to eat, it was nobody's business but our own.

Somehow or the other, my father always seemed to make a way. He might have sold some vegetables from his garden, done a few hours work cutting somebody's lawn, cleaned the cobwebs off someone's ceiling, or even sold some of his crafts made from bamboo and coconut shells, but ultimately, there would be something to eat when I got home for lunch.

My clothes were mostly hand-me-downs which never really seemed to fit right, and I realized from a very tender age that I really did not fit in. I was different. My parents did not have much, but were faithful in tithing and giving to the Lord. My mother especially loved giving to ministries, and I would think, "Why is she sending money to R.W. Shamback, Oral Roberts, and others when we could barely buy food?!" Looking back, I realize it was because my parents knew the Scriptures and looked every day to the hills from where they received their help. (Psalms 121:1)

They woke us kids up, my three brothers, my sister who was the oldest, and me early every morning for family prayer and scripture reading. My siblings and I did not care to do it, but had no choice but to comply. We were already going to church seven days a week - no kidding! They loved God with all their heart and were so in love with the word of God that it was written all over the house. I even memorized several chapters from the Psalms just by hearing my father recite them day after day. I found myself praying for those things that I needed, such things like underwear, shoes, even a dollar or two, to buy myself a bag of popcorn and a drink when my school had a field day at the park. I did not know it then, but I had started to fight the good fight of faith.

As a Christian, your faith is going to be tried on a daily basis, and how you respond determines whether you win that fight or not. In this book I want to encourage you to continue to fight the good fight of faith. If you haven't started yet, you have already wasted too much of life's precious time, so come on! Let's get the ball rolling.

I want to invite you to take this journey with me where I will share with you several situations that I found myself in, which impacted my life and challenged me even more to stay in the fight. It is not easy, especially when you are going through it, but when it is all finished, you are bound to look back and wonder why you didn't realize earlier that it was going to be all right.

My goal for this book is to evangelize and to touch hearts and souls in such a profound way that it will cause a domino effect, which in turn will impact other lives. This book is for everyone. We all encounter struggles on a daily basis and we fight to keep our sanity, to pay the bills, to do well on our jobs, to keep the family together and so much more... But I want to get to the very core of the fight that we are in, and to produce and implement ways to stay in the fight and be successful.

I know for a fact that there are ladies and gentlemen, boys and girls, who have been molested, raped, abused and have been made to feel inferior. They have kept the hurt, guilt and pain bottled up inside because they don't feel like there is anyone that they could confide in or who they feel can be trusted with their secret. Somehow, these survivors may think that they are partly to blame because they loved the person who hurt them, or they think that they might have encouraged their abusers' advances because of the way that they dressed or by being flirtatious. Then again, these courageous souls might have been innocent bystanders, just trying to live life as best as they knew how, only to find themselves caught up in a whirlwind of events that somehow tried to dictate their futures.

Are you one of these beloved souls?

I want to let you know that regardless of how these situations were orchestrated, that you are not responsible for what ensued. You who feel like you can't take it anymore; you who thought of suicide; you who hurt yourself by cutting your body, using your body as a sexual instrument, abusing drugs, and not knowing your worth - this book is for YOU.

This book is also for the abuser who does not realize the emotional, physical, psychological, mental, spiritual and all the other traumas that you have caused your victims while you go about your life as usual. These survivors are haunted by flashbacks that they wish could be erased from their memory forever. They are constantly forced to relive terrifying moments brought about by some kind of trigger that sneaks up on them without warning. All because of you.

Some of you abusers have yet to acknowledge what you have done. You have offered no apology, you've shown no remorse, but guess what? It is not too late to do so. You would be amazed that someone might be waiting for just three words, and these three words could be so powerful that they could practically heal the wounds inflicted by your actions:

"I am sorry."

It could be a matter of life and death. Who knows, you yourself might be living with guilt and regret. The apology would help you, too.

My friend, you need to know that there is also hope for you. There is a man called Christ Jesus that can turn your life around. Read 2 Corinthians 5:17: "Therefore if any man be in Christ, he is a new creature: old things are passed away; behold all things are made new".

Come on! Come all. You are in for a treat. I pray the anointing on every word, every page from the front to the back of this book, and then some. I pray that whosoever reads this book will encounter the transforming power of

God in their lives so that they will never be the same again. I declare healing, deliverance, salvation, restoration and victory in the name of Jesus.

You will not regret having bought this book. As a matter of fact, you will not only tell your friends and comrades to buy it, you will also buy a ton and give them as gifts. Amen.

Chapter 1

THE FIGHT

At some point in our lives, each and every one of us will find ourselves in a fight, be it at home, work, school, with our families, with our friends, neighbors, or kids, you name it, there will be a fight.

As Christians, once we have accepted Jesus in our hearts and lives, we automatically enter into a fight. But it's not just a fight, it's warfare. Ephesians 6:10 admonishes us to be strong, not in our own strength, but in the power of God's strength. Verse 11 tells us to get dressed as a soldier in battle, not putting on our own clothing or gear, but the whole armor of God. When we have this armor on, we are able to prevail in the fight. The amazing thing about this fight is that we are not fighting against flesh and blood (verse 12) but against principalities, against powers, against the rulers of darkness of this world and against spiritual wickedness in high places.

These are a lot of forces that are against us and strive to see us defeated. Even though we do not fight against flesh and blood, God uses individuals to execute certain tasks. We are fighting the spiritual warfare, and are fighting against principalities, powers of darkness, evil demons that disguise themselves through corrupt music, homosexuality, adultery, pornography, masturbation, liquor, drugs, lies, low self-esteem, hatred, jealousy, depression, suicidal thoughts, unforgiveness… and the list goes on and on.

1

We must always be on guard and ready for these spiritual attacks. If we are unprepared, we are going to be bombarded with tests and trials. There are going to be good days when we win the battle almost seamlessly and bad days when we barely survive to limp home and rest from our wounds. There will be days when our faith will be severely tested, and it is at these crucial times - when we feel hopeless, despondent and it seems like there is no light at the end of the tunnel - that we need to cry and pray, weep and mourn, sing and worship. It might seem as if nothing is changing, but this is when our faith comes into focus. We now have no choice but to believe and hope for those things which we cannot see with the natural eye. We have to exercise our faith in God that He is orchestrating people and situations that will ultimately catapult us towards those things we stand in need of and toward our destiny.

Chapter 2

BE DRESSED FOR THE FIGHT

Ephesians 6:11 states, "Put on the whole armor of God that ye may be able to stand against the wiles of the devil".

It is amazing how a person can tell the fight that you are in just by the way you are dressed.

There is a specific attire for each sport, i.e., wrestling, boxing, running, baseball, tennis, and swimming. There is also a dress code for different occupations, such as nurses, firefighters, police officers, chefs, and doctors. We as Christians are also assigned a uniform which protects us from head to toe. I will explain and emphasize the importance of each piece of the attire designed specifically and personally for us by our Heavenly Father.

I see a vast majority of church folks dressing like the world and it is very difficult to identify those who belong to Christ from those who belong to the devil. Yes, there are those who belong to the devil. We hope that it would not be for too long, but the Bible clearly states that you are servants to whom you obey (Romans 6:16).

I am a servant of God, therefore I obey God and follow him. Saint John 10:4 states, "His sheep knows His voice."

Sometimes we find ourselves in dark places in life and we feel like we are all alone. We perceive that no one cares, but then the voice of Jesus breaks through the gloom and whispers soothing words of love and encouragement that steers us through those tough times. One of my favorite scriptures is Hebrews 13:5. The latter part states, "I will never leave thee nor forsake thee". It brings me great comfort when I am going through difficult times, especially when the temptations of the world are upon me.

It's the world's temptations to fit in and do what everybody else is doing that seduces some Christians to dress in a way that overly exposes their bodies. Dresses, blouses and pants so tight they leave nothing to the imagination. Tattoos covering the entire body (having tattoos is not a sin, for Isaiah 49:16 tells us that Jesus has us written in the palm of his hands, but we have to realize that we represent Christ and that our bodies are his temple - so what or who do we depict when we get all those tattoos and piercings?) Some people had these tattoos before they came to know Christ, but I'm just saying! I know this could be said about a number of other things like smoking, drinking, gambling, overeating and such, but I can assure you that as we read the word of God and seek His face, He will show us the things that we need to get rid of, and the habits that need to be broken.

Chapter 3

THE WHOLE ARMOR OF GOD

Ephesians 6:13-18 states, "Therefore take up the whole armor of God, that you may be able to withstand in the evil day, and having done all, to stand firm. Stand therefore, having fastened on the belt of truth, and having put on the breastplate of righteousness, and, as shoes for your feet, having put on the readiness given by the gospel of peace. In all circumstances take up the shield of faith, with which you can extinguish all the flaming darts of the evil one; and take the helmet of salvation, and the sword of the Spirit, which is the word of God, praying at all times in the Spirit, with all prayer and supplication. To that end keep alert with all perseverance, making supplication for all the saints."

We are admonished to take the whole armor of God. We are in a fight, and it is not okay to take a few pieces here and there and leave off the rest. We often complain that "oh, this is too heavy", "this does not look cool", and "what will my friends say or think?" We figure that when we are around our friends and co-workers that we need to fit in.

When they are talking about how they're going to dress for the party, they will think you're old-fashioned if no cleavage is showing or some leg isn't on display or buttocks hanging out of the back of your pants.

I understand, but let me tell you what I've come to know the hard way: if I can't have on the whole armor of God around my friends, then I need to check myself or I need to find some new friends.

The armor of God provides full coverage so that we are able to withstand the attacks of the enemy. We don't need to give the enemy any opening in our armor or loophole in our daily living. We need to be able to withstand all of his attacks in these evil days. The word of God is practical and it would just stand to reasoning that if we get dressed in a certain outfit every day that we automatically know how to dress. There is a saying that goes "practice makes perfect". The more you dress yourself in the armor of God, the more comfortable you will feel, and the more natural it will become. You will not have to wonder what to wear each day because you'd already have it picked out. You'll have laid it out and put it on so many times that no adjustments will need to be made. And it'll be just your size and fit perfectly every time.

In the Bible, David wore the whole armor of God when he went to fight Goliath, David knew that King Saul's armor was not his fit. Too much weight and stress were associated with that armor. The Bible was specific when it said the whole armor of **God.** Not my pastor's armor, not my best friend's armor, not my daddy or mommy's armor, but God's armor. He had it custom made just for you. When you wear the whole armor of God, you are able to stand firm because your feet are planted on the solid rock [Christ Jesus]. You will not be swayed by every wind of doctrine, or by the cunning craftiness of the enemy as he lies in wait to deceive.

God's armor is for our protection: "That we henceforth be no more children, tossed to and fro, and carried about with every wind of doctrine, by the sleight of men and cunning craftiness whereby they lie in wait to deceive". (Ephesians4:14)

We must be aware of who we are fighting against. We are fighting against that old Satan, that liar, that deceiver, that old brut of hell. We are not fighting against our brothers and sisters, our coworkers, children, our husbands or wives, but the devil. He sometimes uses these people as a camouflage to execute his devious schemes, and we neglect most of the times to identify the real culprit behind the whole mess. We need to be able to withstand in these evil days. The word of God is practical.

~~~

When you wear the whole armor of God, you are able to stand firm

~~~

Chapter 4

TRUTH

Ephesians 6:13 gives us the next part of our armor, "having your loins girt about with truth".

The center core of everything should be truth. The scripture uses the words "girt about", which simply means to be fitted closely and snugly, just as a parent swaddles a newborn baby. It is as if the blanket that is used to swaddle the baby has become one with the baby. Wherever the baby goes, the blanket goes. The blanket represents truth and should be with us wherever we go.

Jesus is the way, the truth and the life. He is always present and so we need to be faithful and trustworthy ambassadors.

Truth should come naturally. You don't have to think about truth. You should not have to think about whether or not to tell the truth or a lie to get out of a sticky situation. You cannot use truth as a security blanket only when you need it, but let truth be the very core of who you are.

I remember an April Fools' Day, quite a few years ago when I was working in the operating room (OR) as a surgical tech. There was this amazingly nice surgeon, and my coworkers wanted to play a joke on him. They wondered who they could get to trick him, and unfortunately, I picked the short straw. It was agreed that I would say to him, "Doctor, I cannot work with you anymore because you really hurt my feelings by being mean to me." They chose me because they knew I told the truth, was trustworthy, and there would be no doubt that he would believe whatever I said to him. I begged them not to make me do it, but everyone wanted to trick him to see his reaction, and they all agreed that I was the best person for the job. They finally wore me down and I did it. There were even tears in my eyes, not because I was such a good actress, but because I felt terrible deep inside, to pull a prank on such a sweet and pleasant surgeon.

I did it, and the doctor believed me of course. He was frantic to know in what way he had done me wrong. I pretended to be too distraught to even answer him, so he asked the other nurses and they invented their own story of what he had done to me, all agreeing that he had been real mean to me. They allowed him to digest this sad, ugly, untrue story for about half an hour, and then shouted out "Happy April Fools' Day"!

I truly felt horrible inside, and although it was a joke, I had allowed my loins to become unwrapped. I worried whether the doctor would be able to truly trust me again? Time revealed the answer to be what I expected: not completely.

Truth is a very important piece of our armor. Have you ever come in contact with a person who lies so much that even when they are telling the truth, you don't believe them? You take everything they say with a grain of salt, and you definitely have no confidence in them.

I bring to mind an incident that involved my daughter. It was a Saturday morning and I looked everywhere for my cell phone and could not find it. I remembered last having it in my bedroom, and I had not gone out for the day. My daughter had gone to the movies with a friend, and when I she came back, I asked her if she had seen my phone and she said no. I'd asked her because she had the habit of taking my phone and using it because she did not have one of her own. I figured the phone must have grown some legs and just walked off, because I didn't think it could just disappear in thin air.

I repeatedly asked my daughter, and with tears in her eyes she denied taking the phone. I was wondering if I was losing my mind. An hour or so later, I received a call on the home phone stating that someone had found my phone in the movie theater and because I did not have a lock on it, they called the most often called number. Isn't that something! If they hadn't found my phone, I would still be wandering if it had just disappeared into thin air. And my daughter would have had to live with the lie she told, wearing her spirit down.

Girt yourself with truth every day regardless to the repercussions, or how many friends you might lose. The Bible concludes in John 8:33 that the truth shall set you free.

The most amazing truth is found in John 3:16. "For God so loved the world, that he gave his only begotten son, that whosoever believe it on him, should not perish, but have everlasting life".

Choose Jesus, choose truth, and choose everlasting life and peace.

Chapter 5

THE BREASTPLATE OF RIGHTEOUSNESS

A breastplate in warfare is used to protect the heart. In Proverbs 4:23 it admonishes us to guard the heart, for out of it are the issues of life. If you have ever gotten your heart broken, you will truly know why it is important to wear this piece of armor. For those of you who have not experienced heartbreak, it feels like someone pierced you through the heart with a very sharp sword or knife, continually twisting and turning it until the very breath leaves your body. You are left as a shadow of your former self, walking around like a zombie, and all you can think about is that hurt and the pain.

Heartbreak can be caused between a husband and wife, girlfriend and boyfriend, two friends, or between two people bond by strong trust. Sacrifices have been made, all has been given, and things you really didn't care to do, but because of your love and devotion for that person, you counted it as nothing to grant that person's desires. Never in your wildest dreams would you have thought that that particular person could betray you as they did, but unfortunately they did, and you still have the scars to prove it. You have now decided that you will not be hurt like that again, and have developed a hard shell to protect your heart. You will never let anyone else come close. Your defense is already built up; it is like water running off a duck's back. The barrier cannot be penetrated.

Now imagine that the person who hurt you represents Satan. Although it seems like a negative example, follow me for a moment. Satan only has one desire and that is to sift you like wheat (Luke 22:31). He wants to penetrate your heart and soul and break it into so many pieces that there won't be anything left. You must harden your heart to protect it from Satan's advances. You must build up your defenses, make it so Satan's efforts run off your back like the water on the proverbial duck's back. We are in warfare and we need to wear that breastplate. It is a breastplate of righteousness.

In Proverbs 14:34 it states that "righteousness becomes a nation, but sin is a reproach to any people". When no one is looking, we should still have on that breastplate of righteousness. When you feel like you want revenge, I beseech you: don't take off the breastplate of righteousness. When those who profess Christ and are in the same fight as you are and you look and see that they have stripped themselves of the breastplate of righteousness, grab hold of your breastplate and pull it closer to your body.

We are living in the last days where the word of God declares that "some will depart from the faith, giving heed to seducing spirits and doctrines of devils". (1 Timothy 4:1)

Stay in the fight and live a righteous and godly life. Everywhere you go, spread the gospel by the life you live, by your speech, and by your attitude. Do not be that Christian who people are afraid of approaching who get offended by everything, big or small, even they are asking inconsequential things, such as asking how they are doing.

Chapter 6

PEACE

Have your feet shod with the preparation of the gospel of peace.

The gospel of peace is good news. This is a process - that is why the Scripture refers to it as "preparation".

You might have peace in your family, but no peace on the job. You may have peace at school, but none at church. Peace takes constant preparation.

You might have left the house on your way to work, prepared for what the day might bring forth, prayed and read your Bible, meditated, and sung praises unto God. But before you reached your destination, something happened to disrupt your peace. Your shoelace came undone. Someone cut you off, almost ran you over, and had the nerve to act like it was your fault! All of a sudden, you want to express yourself with nonverbal gestures, but the preparation of peace saves you. Instead of saying or doing something you'd later regret, you say, "God bless you, have a nice day!"

As much as possible, live peaceably with all men, especially those of the household of faith. (Galatians 6:10)

This Scripture means that even in the church you will meet opposition and face those who seek to distract you from your goal. I am telling you, sometimes it is hard to be at peace with some who profess to be Christians. You expect if they profess to be saved, sanctified, and filled with the blessed Holy Spirit, that they will act right and be right, expecting a whole lot more from them than the unsaved. Let me tell you something here: we have to realize that the enemy will use whoever, whenever, and in whatever situation if that person gives him that opening. When these situations arise, we as people of faith who have been prepared with the gospel of peace, should not see the individuals but the spirit that is trying to cause havoc in the church and in the lives of the believers.

In life, you are going to encounter different situations. Just like the weather, it is not always going to be sunshine. When the weather changes and it gets cold outside, you have to put on your thick socks and snow boots so your feet don't get cold and frozen. Spiritually speaking, this analogy relates to the times in your life when you become cold in your attitude and cold in your spirit because it seems that someone or circumstance has pushed you headfirst into a mountain of snow, continually blasting you with snowballs. You try to get up, but you keep falling back down. You are cold and tired and you just pray that the attack will soon be over so that you can warm your frostbitten feet by the fire, but it just keeps going on and on and on.

On the other hand, there are times when you're wearing sandals because it is warm outside and everything is going your way, but then when you least expect it, you stub your toe! My God, what excruciating pain! You hop on one leg, you can't walk straight, you need a crutch, you are bleeding, and you are in pain. Your brothers and sisters in Christ, instead of helping you up, are talking about you. They ignore you even though they see that you are in need of cleansing, could use a little ointment, some clean bandages and overall just a little love.

In both situations – hot and cold - you are hurting, yet you are healing for you are still in the fight! You didn't give up because you are "fighting that good fight of faith". (1Timothy 6:12). With God's help, you begin to form new skin, new flesh, thaw out, and get stronger. You don't feel like exhibiting peace, but you prepare yourself daily anyway, asking God for strength to be at peace with those who saw you fall and did not help you up, and even with those who pushed you down. You have to work right along with them, but now through your experience you can strengthen and encourage someone else who falls because you have been there and done that!

Daily you have to ask God to keep you humble so that you don't do what others did to you; you don't fall into the same trap.

You know what? I think we need to wear those steel toe boots of peace, whether things are going our way or not and let the peace of God, which passes all understanding, keep our hearts and mind. (Philippians 4:7)

The word also states in John 14:27 that "my peace I leave with you, my peace I give to you; not as the world gives do I give to you. Let not your heart be troubled, neither let it be afraid." Armed with this scripture, when people despitefully use you, you can still be at peace with

17

them. Just keep in mind: "render evil for evil onto no man". (1 Peter3:9)

Chapter 7

THE SHIELD OF FAITH

"Taking the shield of faith whereby ye are able to quench all the fiery darts of the wicked." (Ephesians 6:16)

I got a revelation about the shield of faith some time ago and it just blew my mind. This revelation was so awesome that I just kept saying, "Oh my God, oh my God".

It gives me great pleasure to share what the Lord revealed to me.

The shield of faith has three basic components or qualities:
1. It is liquid
2. It is invisible
3. It is solid.

1. Liquid

It shall be able to "quench all the fiery darts of the wicked".

When the enemy throws his fiery darts at you, your liquid shield of faith, will quench (or put out) the fiery, blazing darts.

The word of God has the power to wash, clean, and purify. "That he might sanctify and cleanse it by the washing of water by the word." (Ephesians 5:26) You have to accept the word of God by faith that it will do exactly what it says it will do. Scriptures states that, "faith comes by hearing, and hearing by the word of God." (Romans10:17) Having that assurance that the word of God is all-powerful and will never fail, standing on the firm foundation of this knowledge that "heaven and earth shall pass away" but God's words stands firm and secure. (Matthew 24:35)

Used effectively, your shield of faith is a well of life to you, but also a sea of destruction against the enemy.

This was clearly played out when the children of Israel came in contact with the Red Sea. It became walls on either side of them so that the children of Israel could pass through, but collapsed and drowned Pharaoh's army. The adversary, the devil aims his darts of fire at us children of God, but by the awesome power of God they come in contact with the shield of faith that has the ability to transform right before our very eyes! That liquid shield will quench all those fiery darts and leave the enemy limp, powerless, and confused.

2. *Invisible*

Like the wind, faith is invisible. You cannot see it, but you know when you have it. "Faith is the substance of things hoped for, the evidence of things not seen." [Hebrews 11:1]

At the time that you are exercising your faith the evidence is not seen. You would not have to produce faith if you already possess something that you need. It definitely would not make any sense to hope for something that you already have! Romans 8:24

The Holy Spirit is like the wind. You cannot see him, yet you sense his amazing presence as he manifests himself in your life, and the lives of individuals around you. Without a shadow of a doubt, it will be evident that the Holy Spirit is definitely at work. Thank God for the Holy Spirit that promises to "lead and guide us into all truth." (John 16:13)

Imagine that you are blind and lost. Someone wants to get you to your destination, but instead of taking your arm and guiding you forward, he gives you a set of directions. It is now up to you to step out in faith. You already have directions, but you can't see. Stepping out in this scenario requires trust, i.e., blind faith.

The Holy Spirit is that person who wants to lead you to your destiny. We do it in blind faith as we depend on him for our sight. "When the Holy Ghost is come upon you, you shall have power" (Acts 1:8) This is the power to live right, power to talk right, and power to walk right.

3. Solid

"Above all, taking the shield of faith."

The word "taking" suggests action. "Taking" does not suggest a one-time movement, but constant motion. Remember: the shield of faith is liquid, invisible, yet solid.

Does anything come to mind when you think of these three components together? Well, what about water!

Water is clear and transparent, so I would suggest that it is invisible in its purest form. Water turns from a liquid into a solid, i.e., ice at a temperature of about 32° F (or 0° C).

A great example of faith in action is the sinking of the Titanic. You might say, "Are you crazy lady? How is the sinking of the Titanic faith in action?" That iceberg was there, but was not seen until it was too late. The combination of liquid, solid, and invisible took down "the Unsinkable Ship", that great mountain of steel, when it went into action. That is how powerful faith is when activated!

Above all, in taking the shield of faith, one must have all three forms for the shield to be totally effective. Never leave home without it and have them on all the time. Sleep in them, wake up with them, and live in them. "Without faith it is impossible to please God." (Hebrews 11:6)

Not taking the shield of faith is like a painter going out to paint and not taking his paintbrush, a surgeon going to surgery without his scalpel, and a firefighter going toward a blazing inferno without a water hose. Need I go on?
One more thing about the shield of faith: you not only have to take it, but you also have to use it, and use it effectively. Because faith without works is dead, you might as well have left it at home for all the good it will do you if you don't put it into action.

Hallelujah! Praise be to God! I feel that in my spirit.

To sum it up, the shield of faith is liquid and puts out the enemy's fire; and invisible like water to confuse the enemy because it's the evidence of things not seen. (Hebrews11:1) We do not know how situations will work out, but we just activate our faith and the enemy falls into the sea. I can imagine the devil saying, "I thought I had a clear target, I did not see that wall of water or that patch of ice!"

Trust God and allow him to fight your battles. He will manipulate water, turn it to a solid and transform it into ice barricades when a firm barrier is needed. Praise be to God!

~~~

Trust God and allow him to fight your battles

~~~

Chapter 8

THE HELMET OF SALVATION

Take the helmet of salvation. (Ephesians 6:17)

When does a person put on a helmet? When there is imminent danger of injury to the head.

Protecting the head is essential, it is why race car drivers, bicycle riders, those who ski, boxers, and military personnel wear headgear. As Christians, the enemy tries to mess with our minds by causing us to doubt and to become discouraged when things don't seem to go our way. We feel like a driver whose car spins out of control and heads towards a tree, oncoming traffic, a cliff, or certain life-threatening danger. We feel that we have no control over the situation, thereby causing us to become fearful. When that happens it is only the imps of hell trying to plant seeds of doubt and fear in our minds.

One thing is for sure: we need not fear any situation when we put on our helmet of salvation. For the word of God clearly reminds us that, "God has not given us the spirit of fear, but of power, of love and of a sound mind." (2 Timothy 1:7)

Salvation is our headgear of protection. We accept Christ into your lives by faith, so it is that we walk by faith and not by sight. (2 Corinthians 5:7) Our world may seem

25

to be crashing down around us, but we have precious promises from God. One of which says, "He will never leave us nor forsake us." (Hebrews 13:5) And another is that, "The Lord is my light and my salvation; whom shall I fear? The Lord is the strength of my life, of whom shall I be afraid?" (Psalms 27:1).

As I was writing this chapter, I had a revelation: of all the five senses, four originate in the head. Seeing, hearing, tasting, and smelling all come from the head! When it pertains to salvation, all of these senses come into focus and are activated. We are admonished and encouraged to use these senses intentionally and fully.

Seeing – "O taste and see that the Lord is good. Blessed is the man that you trusted in him." (Psalm 34:8)

Hearing - "Behold I stand at the door and knock: if any man hear my voice and will open the door, I will come in and sup with him, and he with me." (Revelation 3:20)

Tasting – "O taste and see that the Lord is good." (Psalms 34:8)

Smelling - "And walk in love, as Christ also hath loved us, and hath given himself for us an offering and a sacrifice to God for a sweet smelling savor." (Ephesians 5: 2)

The head contains the brain which is the control center of the body. Any injury to the head can cause the whole body to malfunction or function differently. Head injuries can cause comas, blurred vision, confusion, memory loss, breathing problems - you name it. And if the mind is not functioning properly, then the rest of the body fails also.

In other words, as it is in the physical, so it is also in the spiritual.

So do you see now why the helmet of salvation is such an important gear? If the enemy can mess up your head, then you are practically done for. You are left in a state of confusion not knowing whether you are coming or going. The helmet of salvation is our protection to keep our head intact.

"Remember brethren, whatsoever things are true, whatsoever things are honest, whatsoever things are just, whatsoever things are pure, whatsoever things are lovely, whatsoever things are of good report; if there be any virtue, and if there be any praise, think on these things." (Philippians 4:8) To think good thoughts will bring good results. Satan wants us to harbor jealousy, envy, bitterness, unforgiveness, greed and hatred but these things do not edify, but rather hinder us from achieving and receiving all that God has for us.

Our sins were already paid for by the blood of Jesus when he gave his life for us, when he took that analogous car crash in our place which would have left us in a vegetative state. Thank God he has given us the helmet of salvation; all we need to do is to put it on daily. We cannot be afraid to let the world know that we have been bought with a price, and that it is the blood of Jesus Christ. (1 Corinthians 6:20) We are now heirs and joint heirs with him.

If you are not sure of your status as pertaining to the family of God, repeat John 3:16:

"For God so loved the world, that he gave his only begotten son, that whosoever [which includes me] believes on him, shall not perish [no crash and burn for me because I have the helmet of Salvation] but have everlasting life."

If you believe this to be true say, "Lord Jesus, I am a sinner. Forgive me of my sins, come into my heart, and save my soul. I now accept you as my Savior."

Congratulations, you have accepted the gift of salvation!

Chapter 9

THE SWORD OF THE SPIRIT

We are in a fight. Better yet, we are in warfare.

We are equipped with our weapons, which is the sword of the spirit. You might say "people don't fight with swords anymore, that it is outdated; it goes back to medieval times". Yes, we now use more high-tech weapons such as guns, bombs, grenades and other explosives. But do not underestimate the sword of the spirit. This sword is a very special kind, like no other. It can both cut and heal at the same time. It is sharper than any other two edged sword. It has the ability to eradicate your enemies when used properly. Yet this very same sword can be used on yourself to heal by "piercing through soul and the spirit, joints and marrow", cauterizing or burning out the things which have become diseased and contaminated. (Hebrews 4:12)

This sword even knows what people are thinking and what they intend to do. Wow! Isn't that amazing? A sword that knows what your opponent is planning, knows what his next move is, and is able to strategically maneuver your actions so that you can avoid the pitfalls of the adversary. What a great weapon to have in battle, to know your rival's next move before he makes it. That's what the word of God does, which is our sword of the spirit. When we encounter the enemy and his tactics, the word of God, which we have hidden in our hearts (Psalms 119:11) for such a time as this, rises to the surface and completes its mission.

Jesus, after he had fasted 40 days and 40 nights, was tempted of the devil. Satan, thinking that Jesus was weak, offered him bread. But Jesus, even though he might've been weak in the flesh, was strong in the spirit, and proceeded to let that liar know that man shall not live by bread alone, but by every word that proceeds out of the mouth of God. (Luke 4:4)

Jesus used that two edged sword on the devil, and he had no other choice than to scamper away like a dog with his tail between his legs. (Matthew 4:1 – 11) Notice that the devil left him, but it was only for season. This means that he will show up again, so we have to be always ready with the word of God - The sword. We do not know which direction the devil will come from, or what kind of temptation he may try to bring our way so we have to be always ready.

Be aware and understand that the enemy also knows scriptures, and he will use them to suit his purpose. When we know the word of God for ourselves, and how to test the spirit (1 John 4:1), we will have discernment and be able to beat the devil at his own game. Please know that you have to take special time out to study the word of God. It is not enough to just listen to the preacher on Sunday mornings, or to attend Bible study; you need to read the Bible for yourself also.

You cannot get bored reading the word of God, for the Bible is full of interesting characters and it incorporates all types of genres. You want a mystery? It has it. Poetry? It's there in abundance. Drama? There's plenty of it. You want to know about nutrition and the right foods to eat? Look no further. Basically, the Bible should be our Internet, the place where we go when we have questions that need to be answered, guidance when we need direction, wisdom to know when God is correcting us, insight into what's happening in our world and what we can expect.

The Bible is the most popular book on the planet and has all the answers to life's problems. Someone once said that the letters of the word BIBLE stand for Basic Instructions Before Leaving Earth. I take that to mean that we have to consult this book on a daily basis to ensure we are living right and adhering to the guidelines written therein. The word of God should challenge us to be more like Him every day. Unfortunately, like children, we don't always do what's right. So we shouldn't be surprised when we are chastised now and then. All scripture is God-breathed and is useful for teaching, correcting and training in righteousness, so that the servant of God may be thoroughly equipped for every good work. (2 Timothy 3:17)

I beseech you again to study the word of God for it was there in the beginning. In the beginning was the word, and the Word was with God, and the Word was God. (John 1:1) And it will be there till the end: "Heaven and earth will pass away, but my words will never pass away." (Matthew 24:35)

I would like to tell you a few more wonderful things about the word of God. The word of God is a lamp unto our feet and a light onto our path. (Psalms 119:105) The word of God is quick and powerful, and is sharper than any two-edged sword. (Hebrews 4:12). And last, but not least, if we hide the word of God in our hearts, we will not sin against God. (Psalm 119: 11)

When we study the word of God, we will know what God likes and does not like, and what He expects of us.

Chapter 10

PRAYING ALWAYS: PREVAILING IN PRAYER

Notice that prayer is not part of the armor, but it is essential to our victory.

What is prayer anyway?

I would liken prayer to five objects.

1. Prayer is the **master key**: It unlocks the chains of darkness and sets the captives free. An example is Paul and Silas in Acts 16:16-40 where they prayed while in jail and caused the earth to quake, thus releasing their chains. Through their prayer, the jailer and his whole family came to know God and His wonder-working power. Prayer unlocks every door, and even closes those that need to be closed.

2. Prayer is a **mirror**: It shows us ourselves and what we need cleaned up and straighten up. James 1:22-25. We speak to God and He speaks back to us. Now what good is it if when we look into the mirror and see something that needs to be fixed, but we do not fix it, or needs to be cleaned and we do not clean it? What good does it for us? Not a thing. Make sure when God tells you what adjustments you need to make, that you are obedient.

3. Prayer is a **watch tower**: It shows us the condition of those who are lost and opens our spiritual eyes to see clearly. Clear sight allows us to throw out a lifeline to those who perish. They could be our families, our co-workers or our loved ones. In fact, we may not even know them at all, but we see the need for salvation. See Isaiah 21:8 & Habakkuk 2:1.

4. Prayer is a **covering**: Like an orange peel, it protects you, and without it, you begin to dry up. Seven days without prayer makes one weak. And just as a mother hen hides her chicks under her wings, so too does the Lord covers us and protect us with his blood. Psalms 91:4 says, "He shall cover thee with his feathers and under his wings shall thou trust." It is essential to cover yourself and your family in prayer every day, before setting out on your various assignments.

5. Prayer is a **treasure chest**: Whatever we need is available to us through prayer and supplication, for God's word says that "if we seek that we shall find". (Matthew 7:7) We must always search diligently for treasure, follow guidelines (Bible), and be consistent in order to gain the prize. We just said that we had to seek, but what are we seeking? In order to get what we desire, we have to play by the rules. So we have to "seek first the kingdom of God and his righteousness," (Matthew 6:33) and then and only then will every other thing be added to us. Yes, prayer is a treasure chest, but you have to seek his face first and not his hand. I would also like you to remember that prayer incorporates the list below:

- Promise – "yea and Amen": For all the promises of God in him are yea, and in him Amen, unto the glory of God by us. 2 Corinthians 1:20.

- Resource – "the cattle on a thousand hills": For every beast of the forest is mine, and the cattle upon a thousand hills. Psalms 50:10.

- Ammunition – "the weapons of our warfare are not   carnal": For the weapons of our warfare are not carnal, but   mighty   through   God   to the pulling down of strong holds 2 Corinthians 10:4

- Youth – "renew": Who satisfieth thy mouth with good things; so that thy youth is renewed like the eagle's. Psalms 103:5

- Eyes – "vision": I will lift up mine eyes unto the hills, from whence cometh my help. Psalms 121:1

- Result – "He does all things well": And were beyond measure astonished, saying, He hath done all things well: he maketh both the deaf to hear, and the dumb to speak. Mark 7:37

You cannot fight without prayer. To me, prayer is also like an armored truck with ammunition used in combat. According to Wikipedia, "the armored truck is multifunctional and it is designed to protect and ensure the well-being of the transported individuals and or contents. The armored truck is completely bulletproof and can withstand extreme degrees of heat."

Prayer, like the armored truck, can transport you to your destination, and also offer you protection. One of my favorite scriptures clearly demonstrates the ultimate and unique power of prayer - Psalms 91: 1-7.

He that dwelleth in the secret place of the most high [prayer] shall abide under the shadow of the Almighty. I will say of the Lord, He is my refuge and my fortress: my God in him will I trust. Surely he shall deliver thee from the snare of the fowler and from the noisome pestilence. He shall cover me with his feathers, and under his wings shall thou trust: his truth shall be thy shield and buckler. Thou shall not be afraid for the terror by night, or for the arrow that flieth by day, nor for the pestilence that walketh in darkness, nor for the destruction that wasted at noon day. A thousand shall fall at thy side, and ten thousand at thy right hand but it shall not come nigh thee.

I could go on, but please read the rest of it. It is a beautiful chapter which I often recite in prayer.

***

Have you ever been in a prayer drought? Has there been a time in your life where it seems so difficult for you to pray? You want to pray, but you just seem to allow everything else to take priority? You bring extra work home from the job; you have to fix dinner; then there's the kids, maybe even help with schoolwork; spend time with the spouse; and before you know it is bedtime, and you whisper a little "thank you Lord for taking me through the day" as you drift off to sleep? I believe all of us at some point in our Christian walk have encountered this drought and it goes on for a while, but take heed, rise up, don't allow yourself to get faint and sluggish. Pull yourself up, brush yourself off, plead for the showers of blessing on your thirsty soul, and immerse yourself into God's river of living water.

I have been in the drought and know firsthand that the longer you stay in that drought, the weaker you become.

Allen E. Varlett penned the words "seven days without prayer makes one weak". You may wonder how to get out of this drought. You may think, "I really don't feel like praying, I feel frustrated and my prayers don't seem to be answered." You know what? Prayer is work. Like some of us, we have jobs and at times we don't feel like going, but we get up anyway and go. So it is with prayer: we can't go by feelings, we have to act on faith even when it comes to prayer.

Some of the greatest prayer moments that I have experienced have occurred when I dragged myself into my prayer closet, not feeling at all like praying, but just knowing that I needed to take special time out for the Lord. I remember one Sunday I went to church and I was feeling down and under the weather. I had already determined in my heart that I was not going to take any leading role that day and I was even a little late on purpose to make sure of it. Little did I know that service was running a little behind schedule and I was just in time to be called up to lead praise and worship. As I stood up there, not really wanting to be in that position, I honestly told the church that I did not feel like doing praise and worship, but after thinking of how good God has been to me, and all the times that He came through for me, I asked myself, "How could I not do whatever I am asked to do, and do it in spirit and in truth?" I remember the first song that I lead was "We Bring the Sacrifice of Praise". The Holy Spirit took over in that song and for the rest of the service I remember telling the Lord that I do not want my praise to be a sacrifice, I want to be able to give my praise to him freely, totally and without reservations.

Sometimes when we make sacrifices it hurts, and it's almost like it's dragged out of us. Our praise should not be a sacrifice, it should be a continuous free flow of gratitude and love. Prevailing in prayer takes work, dedication, and a made-up mind. We have to have a Jacob attitude as referenced in Genesis chapters 27 through 35. "Lord I will not let go until you bless me." We are in a fight, so be prepared to receive cuts and bruises, but victory is ours if we persevere. Ephesians 6:12 states that "we wrestle not against flesh and blood but against principalities and powers, against the rulers of the darkness of this world, and against spiritual wickedness in high places". So we are fighting the spiritual battle and need extra spiritual ammunition.

Chapter 11

WATCH AND PRAY

What does it mean to watch and pray? Does it mean that whenever you pray you need to keep your eyes open? Does it mean that you open your eyes every so often when you're in prayer? Even though you can do those things if you choose to, that's not what "watch and pray" means. It simply means that you are to be aware, to be on the alert and on guard for the schemes of the enemy. It also means being attentive to what God is trying to say to you.

Sometimes we get so caught up telling God all about our problems and/or situations that we don't take time to listen to Him. He might want to give the solutions to our problems, steer us in the right direction, or even to let us know that the answer is on the way. But we can't hear Him because we're too busy talking instead of listening.

When we pray, we should look forward to and expect our prayers to be answered. An example of praying but not watching is the story of Peter in Acts 12:14-15 when he was released from prison by an angel. The saints were having a prayer meeting on Peter's behalf, praying for deliverance from prison but when Rhoda, a little girl, came and told them that Peter was at the door, no one believed her. Everyone continued to pray even when their prayers were answered. They were praying, but not expecting the manifestation; praying, but not listening for the answer.

First Peter 5:8 cautions us to "Be sober, be vigilant because your adversary the devil, as a roaring lion, is walking about seeking whom he may devour". We need to be watchful, to be awake and aware, and always be on our guard. We cannot afford to slumber and sleep like the five virgins in Matthew 25. Five of the virgins were wise enough to not only have oil in their lamps, but also on reserve. The other five were close, but unfortunately missed the bridegroom. Another example is when Jesus was about to be crucified. He took his most trusted and dearest disciples who were like his right hand men - Peter, James and John - to the garden of Gethsemane. There he confided in them and let them know that his soul was sorrowful. He then entreated them to watch and pray with him for one hour. Twice he came back and found them sleeping. Yes they were tired, yes they had quite a long day, but they failed to realize that they were in a fight and could not give in to the pleasure of sleep for the enemy is devising and concocting his schemes! You can bet your life that he does not sleep!

Jesus is counting on us, his children, to be always ready and prepared. This fight is not a physical one, but a spiritual one. Knowing that "the weapons of our warfare are not carnal, but mighty in the pulling down of strongholds. (2 Corinthians 10:4)

When things are not going your way, don't give up. Don't be bombarded with doubts and fears. This is the time you must pray even more, and watch God work a miracle in your life. If all you can do is groan and moan, do that to your Heavenly Father. Cry if you must, sing if you can, and even dance like crazy, but do it to the glory of

God. King David did it all, and did not give up, so don't you give up either!

Prayer changes things and prayer changes lives. I want you to know that in this life all of us will go through some tough times. Think of it like a prison you are locked in, feeling hopeless like there is no way out, no escape; but you have a choice. You can stay there and do nothing but murmur and complain; you can try to dream or sleep your way out of it; or you can worship and pray your way out of it. The choice is yours.

Pray during times when it looks hopeless, pray even more then, and remember that there is one who grants pardon to those who are sentenced even to death: Jesus!

You have to watch and pray when the kids are on drugs, having illicit sex, and serving time in jail. Watch and pray when the children won't listen to your advice and ruin their lives with poorly thought out decisions. Watch and pray when there's nothing you can do, when the child slip out and you don't know where he or she is. Watch and pray when you have pain in your heart and it seems like it's too much to bear. Watch and pray when you are a single parent and are raising your children in the fear and admonition of the Lord, yet they turn their backs on God. Watch and pray when the children look for love in all the wrong places. Cast all your cares upon me says Jesus in 1 Peter 5:7.

There really is not much else you can do, so watch and pray.

~~~

Pray during times when it looks hopeless

~~~

Chapter 12

DELIVERED FROM DEPRESSION

I was not diagnosed by a medical doctor, but I know without a shadow of a doubt that I was depressed. I did not care how I dressed or did not dress. I pretended I was all right when I was around people, but when I was alone with myself, I would break down and cry. All I wanted to do was sleep. When I ate, I cried because I thought I was too fat. I cried because I could not prevent myself from eating, for that gave me a little bit of comfort. When I thought about the calories that I was packing on, I cried even more. I was always crying.

Some people lose weight when they are stressed and going through hard times, but me, whoopty-do! I have to eat as if my life depended on it. There was a time that while food was still in my mouth, I'd contemplated what I was going to eat next, and I would just keep right on eating without ever feeling full. The food was like Novocain; it took care of the pain temporarily. But when that wore off, there I was at the same place, right back where I started. What a predicament.

During this period in my life, I did not care about anything. I started to neglect myself. I did not feel like taking a shower, and those that know me, know that I take pleasure in smelling not only good but great. I don't use scents as a cover up, I truly enjoy the whole experience of being clean and smelling good. Perfumes, scented soaps and lotions, powders and lovely smelling bubble baths were and are my pleasures. That was my weakness, so for me not to want to bathe was a sure sign that something was terribly wrong.

I was binge eating, feeling terrible, and crying more. I was overweight and did not know how to get the pounds off. I was raising three kids on my own, did not have much help, and no one to talk to. I remembered an occasion when I took my oldest son to the doctor and things were out of control. The bills were piling up, the kids' father wasn't acting right, I was working two jobs and going to school full time (No wonder I was depressed!) I sat in the doctor's office and as the nurse took my son to get his weight, the doctor began asking me questions such as is everything alright at home, is there any abuse in the home and do you have a support system? I had to be very careful how I answered his questions because although there was no abuse in the house, I felt that he knew something was not right. I told him that I had a cousin who helped me out with the kids and that everything was fine. Shortly after that he left the room and I could feel the tears building up. I was overwhelmed, to say the least. I did not want him to come back and find me crying, but I felt like I was going to lose it. He had cracked that shell and exposed some of my yolk (or issues that I had tried so hard hide).

I was afraid. I did not want my kids taken away from me. I'd had those kids out of wedlock, but I never regretted having them - they were the best thing that ever happened to me (aside from salvation).

A few months later when I was having one of those bouts of depression, I decided to record myself since I didn't have anyone to talk to. I was simply stating how I felt and how life seemed to be so hopeless and there did not seem to be any light at the end of my tunnel. I wanted to die. I wrote a poem during that time that I included at the end of this chapter. When I came to myself, I realized that I had three kids that had no one to depend on but me. They did not ask to be here, but they were, and it was up to me to be the best mother that I could be. It was up to me to provide for them and meet their needs to the best of my ability.

My daughter was probably in second grade when I received a call from a teacher. She was calling to make sure that I was okay. Apparently the class was given an assignment to write about their parents, and seeing that her father was not around, she wrote about me. She'd stated that I did not play with her or take her anywhere, and all I did was sleep. That hurt me to the very core for it was the plain and simple truth in a nutshell. I managed to convince the teacher that I worked nights (which I did) and did chores while they were at school, so I needed to rest in order to go back to work.

That was the turning point in my life as far as the depression was concerned. The child was absolutely correct in her judgment and I knew that things had to change. About two weeks later, I got down on my knees and asked God to help me and take away the depression. I told Him that I couldn't take it anymore and I needed His help to take care of these children.

It happened instantaneously.

I got up off my knees and started singing and dancing. I was so surprised and elated that I got my cassette player and began recording myself and how happy I felt. I rewound the cassette to listen to it and got my previous recording from when I was depressed. My God! What a contrast.

In the first recording, my voice was low and sounded lazy; a tired sort of drawl. I sounded hopeless, sick and pathetic. As I listened to myself, it sounded like a voice that would suck the very air out of the atmosphere and I wondered how I had gotten to that place. If that was the way I sounded those months prior at my son's doctor's appointment, it was no wonder the doctor suspected – probably knew - that I was depressed.

I went on to listen to the second recording, the one I'd just made. When I compared the two, it was like a breath of fresh air. My voice was light and cheerful and full of hope. I had no other option than to thank the Lord as tears streamed down my cheeks, but those were definitely tears of joy. Since then I have never been the same. There were times when I felt like the depression was trying to make a comeback, but immediately I'd stop it in its tracks. I let the devil know in no uncertain terms that I have been healed and delivered and there is no way that he is welcome in my life again in any way, shape or form.

This is the poem I wrote during the time of my depression:

"The Crying Song"

Sometimes I feel like crying, crying, oh!

Would someone help me please?
It's then that I think about dying, dying, no!
Could someone help me please?

I'm just not enough to go around
Enough hours in the day just can't be found
My life is spinning out of control
The cares of life is taking its toll

You wouldn't know unless you are single as I am
You wouldn't know unless you found yourself in a jam
You wouldn't know if you've always had someone to turn to
You wouldn't know what it is like when your world starts to crumble

You may say that doesn't sound so bad,
But have you ever felt like you were going mad?
Feel so all alone,
And have no one to call on the telephone?
Felt like you just wanted to scream and scream,
But hoping you wake up and find it's a dream
Felt like you just wanted to run away and hide
But look down and see three kids by your side?

Two hundred fifty pounds - can't lose the weight,
Five foot two - my God, what a state!
Belly so big was asked when I'm due,
Was so embarrassed I answered in a week or two

Was married to a married man
Who caused me pain and wrecked my van,
Want me to go on, believe me I can,
Even accused me of sleeping with another man

Still can't see why I'd want to die?
But I choose the lesser evil so I cry, cry, and cry.

Don't feel sorry for me, and think I'm a basket case,
For believe it or not I'm now in a better place.
I've let go of all that hurt and pain,
And I've gained control of my life again.
And now and then I cry you see,
But it's all because of the joy in me.

Chapter 13

DELIVERED FROM LOW SELF ESTEEM HATRED AND ABUSE

Low Self-Esteem

I grew up on a small island in the Caribbean called Montserrat. My parents were poor and I felt from a very early age that people looked down their noses at our family. We had no TV and on our way home from church at night, while our parents stopped to talk with the sister from church on her porch, us kids would try to peep through the louvers just to watch her TV. (Louvers were windows or doors made with layers of glass or wooden shutters that could be closed or opened by winding them up or down, like car windows before automatic buttons).

The shows that I remember were "Hawaii 5-0", "Charlie's Angels", and "Gun Smoke". The older children inside the house were in their twenties, and sometimes closed the louvers in our little faces. Looking back now, I could see how they might have seen us as invading their privacy, but back then, it just made me feel that I was less than and had little value. I felt like a nobody.

That memory stayed in my subconscious for years. I had a dream that I was back at that house. Before the dream started I was told that I was going to be invited into the house, but that I should not stay. I was told that after a while I should excuse myself by saying that I had another engagement. I thought that was strange, but then at the end it all made sense.

The family was hosting a dinner at the house and there was a huge table loaded with delicious, mouthwatering foods of all sorts. When it came time to be seated, one of the hostess' daughters who used to close the louvers in our faces directed me to a small, round, rough, and obviously handmade wooden table at the far end of the room. She proceeded to place a plate of food before me and expected me to sit and eat like a beggar. There I was, back home after all that time, having established myself as a professional in the US, and found myself back to this awful place when I was a child. I thought of myself as somebody and was treated as inferior all over again. Tears rolled down my cheeks and I remembered the instructions that I'd been given before the dream, so I said, "Please excuse me, I have to go."

I walked out the room and that was when I woke up. I had cried during my dream; tears were still streaming down my face. As I do with practically every situation, I went to my daddy and asked him to explain it. He held me in his arms and said, "Child, I am preparing a banquet for you and you will be able to feast on the food of your choice. You won't have to worry about someone giving you a chicken wing when you want a leg instead, or serving you a hot dog when you want to eat steak." He continued, "You will be the guest of honor and able to sit at the table with Jesus."

That goes for you also my sister and brother - if you remain faithful in fighting the good fight of faith.

Hatred and Abuse

I was raised in the Pentecostal church, and was at one point the baby of the church. My grand uncle was the pastor and then later after his passing my uncle (my mother's half-brother) became the pastor. Because we were poor, we were not recognized as family so to speak because my mother married someone out of her ranks and therefore was considered an outcast. I was always pleasantly plump, and around the age of 12 I looked like18 compliments of my big breasts, inherited from my mother. "Thanks mom!"

It was then that I realized that grown men in and out the church were looking at me and even tried to molest me, family members included. Once I escaped a cousin's house by jumping out the window after he pulled me to him, and something on his person alert me that I needed to get out of there as fast as I could. Somehow I got wings and I flew. Another time, I was at the beach and had to climb up a tree in order to get away from another individual. Yet another time I was at home and this married man from the church who used to sit on his porch on Saturdays and watch all who passed by (and so probably knew that my parents were not home) came over to my house. He was well respected in the church and would often summon me as I went to the store to buy something for him as a way to get me in his house. Those days even though I knew what his motives were, I could not refuse to go when he called, and only God knew how I escaped those few times with him just fondling my breast. (Not that it was not a big deal, but I knew that it could have been much worse.)

One day I was in my yard washing clothes in a big bath pan when I saw that man park his car in front of our house and walk up the pathway. I quickly ran inside the house, but I knew that he had seen me. I had the feeling that something terrible was about to happen. He was out for blood that day, the most valuable of all blood, the kind that should be given, not taken. Somehow it was like a voice told me to hide behind the front door thus making the triangular cocoon my fortress. I heard him climbing the wooden steps and with each creaking sound my heart seemed to beat louder. He walked right pass me, calling my name, oblivious that his pawn was within reach. I kept silent, not even daring to breath, praying that he would not discover my hiding place. He kept calling my name as he peered through each of the four rooms that were separated only by makeshift curtains. He looked inside and out and inside again, under beds and tables with the earnest intent of a dog sniffing out his prey and all the while calling my name. I believe that it was God who kept my mouth shut and who kept me behind that door where that man could not see me.

He eventually gave up and I did not come out of my hiding place till I heard his car start up and drive away. God protected me that day, and it is why I say, "Don't mess with me, God loves me too much".

I was only 13 when that happened. My overly developed body made me a target for old and young men alike. God kept me safe until I was 16 when I got raped by a friend of the family. I tried running, but that time I was not successful. He locked the door and chased me all around the room, dragging me to the bed. I managed to get up and head for the door again, but he got a hold of me and pinned me to the wall before I could reach it. I found myself suspended in the air and oh the pain! I was literally between a rock and a hard place. At that point I had lost the fight. My blood dripped on the floor and I could not wrestle anymore; that would have helped him and hurt me even more.

He never said he was sorry, and we never discussed it until many years later when I brought up the subject. I had told no one about the attack because I was ashamed and embarrassed. It was years later that I told my sister and my best friend. I held hatred in my heart for a long time. I prayed to God about it and asked Him to take away that uncontrollable feeling. At times I would be okay, but then something would trigger that memory and the hurt would return with a vengeance. I'd want to hurt him in return, but it was like my hands were tied and I was helpless once again. I hated him at intervals, yet he was so far away and was not even aware of how I was feeling. I was going through all of these emotions that I did not know what to do with, did not know how to act, could not talk to anyone about them, so they just piled up. I was even mad at God, and asked, *God, why did you allow this to happen?*

About 30 years later, I got my answer and got delivered. It so happened that my attacker was caught in an embarrassing situation. I tried to help, but to no avail. It was then that the scripture came to mind, "what is man for his days are like grass, as a flower of the field so he flourisheth and the wind passeth over it and it is gone and the place thereof shall know it no more". (Psalm103:15)

A few days later when I thought of the entire situation, I laughed like I had never laughed before and cried at the same time. I felt such a release, a cleansing that soap and water could never accomplish, only possible through the blood of Jesus.

That laughter did me good like a medicine. (Proverbs 17:22) And since then I don't feel like a victim any longer. I actually thank God because He showed me that I was at an age where I could deal with it. There could have been so many different and worst scenarios. I now can tell those who are hurting that the pain and hurt does go away. I tell other survivors that they can experience healing through the power of Jesus Christ. I never thought I could forgive or forget, but yes, it is possible, for with God, all things are possible. Jesus is a deliverer.

I got married to a man who was already married. Of course I did not know that until after we were married. He was very jealous, controlling and ignorant, and because of that he did things and said things just to hurt me. He wrecked my car so that I would have to depend on him for rides to and from work and anywhere else I needed to go. He physically threatened me and even put his hand in my face. That was the last straw; I filed a restraining order and got a divorce. I gave him the opportunity to see his kids, but he chose not to. He has not paid any child support ever and I have no clue whether he is dead or alive after 14 years. But I don't need to know - God has been taking care of me and my kids like no one else could.

I have to say one more time, "Don't mess with me because you don't know just how much God loves me." I don't hate my ex-husband anymore either, nor do I resent him. It is truly well with my soul.

Chapter 14

HAS BEEN A HUSBAND TO ME

There are times in your life when you just know that you and God are like "right here". Your bro, your girl, your pal, your dawg, your best friend. You are on the mountaintop together, like when he took Peter, James and John up to mount of transfiguration and they were so glad to be there. No doubt they wished they could stay there forever.

Well, I was experiencing a season like this, where my prayer life was great, I was reading and studying my Bible, God and I were talking in the car, talking and sharing secrets at work. He was helping me out on the job when there were decisions to make and I didn't know what to do, it felt like He was whispering answers in my ears; we were that close.

I was driving home from work one afternoon, and usually I would have my windows up listening to Praise 102.5, but for some reason, I decided to roll down the windows and turn off the radio. I did this and right away I heard a funny noise. I realized that I had a flat tire. If my windows were up and the music had been on, I would not have realized I had a flat before serious damage had occurred. I was on Freedom Parkway, a very busy freeway in downtown Atlanta. I was just about to get on I-20, and I thought about trying to make it to the next exit where I might find a tire shop, but something or someone said to me, "No, you will only mess up your rims, which will cause you more expense and unnecessary headache." I decided to pull over on the shoulder of the road where I could call my roadside service. I pulled over and was about to dial the number when a pickup truck pulled over in front of me. A white guy built like a construction worker in his mid-thirties came over and asked me if I had a spare tire. I responded yes, and that guy began to change the tire. I wanted to show my appreciation by offering him some money, but he said, "No thanks, I would just like you to remember me in prayer." He said, "My name is Donald and I am going through a difficult time in my life right now."

I said I would pray for him, and I must've been in a state of shock for after he had gone, I said to myself, "Lois, you could have prayed for him right there and then." I remember thinking *God, look at you, before I even asked, you sent someone right away to take care of my needs.* If I had been married, the first person I most likely would have called would have been my husband. So there God was, showing up as a husband to me. The guy that is lucky to marry me sure has some big shoes to fill!

Another day I needed to mow the lawn. It really looked horrible because my lawnmower was not working. It had cranked out the last time I mowed the lawn and I even had to borrow my neighbor's lawnmower to finish. He tried seeing if he could figure out why the lawnmower had stopped working, but could not. It had oil and gas, so he tried to start it to no avail. I tried also, but failed.

My son and I tried several times for the next few weeks, but nothing happened. On this particular day, I said, *Lord, I need the lawnmower to work.* If it didn't, I would get a fine from my homeowners association because the lawn looked so bad. I said, *I don't know anything about lawnmowers but I am going to get some tools from the garage, and tighten here and fiddle there and pray that it would somehow work.*

I went down to the garage and before I got the tools something said to me, *Why don't you try again?* I pulled the string, and was shocked out of my wits when it came on right away on the very first try. Usually I would have to pull it two or three times before it would start. I mowed the entire yard without it cutting off. Before it would cut off when the bag was full and needed to be changed, but that day, I did the whole yard in one go, and it has been working ever since. God was a husband to me that day and also another time when He fixed my washing machine.

This last instance is one of the biggest financial miracles that I have experienced so far, but I expect there will be even greater in times to come.

I was going through the Affordable Home Financing Program and it had been a long, frustrating, nerve-wrecking experience. It seemed like every other week they were threatening to foreclose on my house. I was finally at the end when I needed to prove that I could make three consecutive payments on time to be approved. I was at the last payment which was due in a few days when my paycheck was deposited, but it wasn't going to be enough to cover the mortgage – I had a negative balance of about $200.00. I needed about $500.00 in total to pay the overdraft amount and the mortgage. I worried, I cried and I prayed. I searched every letter, I looked on the ground everywhere I went, prayed that God would speak to someone in the church, I cried and prayed over and over again, I sang songs of hope and faith and the song that seemed to be on the radio to and from work was "I Need You Now" by Smokie Norful. I made that song my anthem morning, noon and night, and every waking hour till the day before the mortgage was due.

I went to work in the operating room (OR), and a male nurse said to me, "Step into my office for a moment," which wasn't an office, but we stepped to the side of the center core where he asked me, "What is your need?"

Those words sounded like they literally proceeded from the mouth of God. Tears filled my eyes and immediately ran down my cheeks because I was overwhelmed I proceeded to tell him my story and he said hold on! He ran down stairs and got $500.00 from the ATM and gave it to me. No strings attached. I knew right away that it was God. Later I asked him if I needed to repay him and he said that when God speaks we have to listen and He told him to give me the money. God works in mysterious ways. The job was the last place that I would have looked to for such a miracle. Isn't He just altogether lovely? He is the best husband ever!

Now having said all that, in a marriage there will come a time when either party could feel hurt because of something that the other person did or failed to do. Well, in this case it's me and Jesus or God, and he never fails, so the failure lies in me. I proved him to be a Jealous God. (Exodus 20:5)

Quite a few years ago, my best friend at the time asked me how I coped with being single and I basically told her that when I felt a certain way that I would keep myself busy and find something to do to keep my mind from entertaining the desire. She went on to say that I should buy myself a toy, that way I won't have to worry about falling into the trap of fornication as I had done before and end up having children out of wedlock. We went out to dinner that night, and without informing me, she pulled up to this adult store and urged me to go in and pick out something. She said that she and her husband used toys in the bedroom so she knew exactly where to go in the store. I picked the first thing that came to my hand because I was embarrassed and wanted to get out of there as quick as possible.

I started using the toy and it started taking up too much of my time. Then one day when I was using that toy down on my knees, I heard the audible voice of God call my name and said, "Lois, don't you know that your body is the temple of the living God?"

God literally scared the "hell" out of me, so I was like, oh my God! I jumped up and got rid of that thing. That was in 2004, and now it is 2018, and no more toys. I'm not married yet, but the Lord has kept me and is still keeping me. I was scared at first and I kept myself pure out of fear that the Lord might cut me off, but as time goes by I realize just how much He loves me, that He spared my life and now I keep myself pure because I could not think of hurting Him or casing Him pain. Like Joseph said when Potiphar's wife tried to seduce him," how could I do such wickedness and sin against my God?" (Genesis 39:9)

He is a loving God, but he also is a jealous God, and a God of wrath who is angry with the wicked every day. (Psalm 7:11) If you are single, ask God to keep you pure because using toys and performing masturbation is not pleasing to God, and only opens a door for the enemy. Sex before marriage is still wrong, regardless of the days we are living in. We are the bride of Christ, so I will encourage you to love him with your whole heart and please him in all you do.

Chapter 15

DON'T MESS WITH ME

"Don't mess with me! You do not realize just how much God loves me."

This might seem like a bold statement to make, and to tell you the truth, I usually do not talk this way. But when it comes to God, and all of the things that He has done for me, and the ways in which He seems to just show up for me, I can't help but join with Psalm 34:2,4 and say, "My soul shall make her boast in the Lord, the humble shall hear thereof and be glad... For I sought the Lord and he heard me, and delivered me from all my fears."

I boast of his forgiveness. I got saved at an early age, around eight or nine, but when I was in my twenties, I felt like life was passing me by. I backslid and had three kids out of wedlock. In spite of that, God still said, "Don't worry girl, I still love you." I tend to relate to that young lady in Ezekiel 16:6 who was polluted in her own blood because when she was born, no one cleaned her up, but rather was left in an open field in all types of weather, amidst all the creepy crawlers. Her naval string had not been cut, she had not been washed but was left for death and destruction. God in his love and compassion, passed by her, cleaned her up and commanded her to live. He fed her, He raised her til she became a beautiful young lady, at which point he decked her with silver and gold and elegant clothing. She was breathtaking, there was no sign of her distasteful beginning. Yet somehow that young woman got caught up in self and pride, and forsook the one who took care of her. Like that child, I had turned my back on God, I had lived my life like a sinner that did not know any better. When I came to myself, I was ashamed, and when I'd come to the end of my rope, I wanted to die. I had made a mess out of my life, but God saw something worthwhile in me, and like that baby girl, washed me clean and gave me a reason for living.

Chapter 16

KNOW YOUR ADVERSARY

Ephesians 6:12 "For we wrestle not against flesh and blood, but against principalities against powers against the rulers of the darkness of this world, against spiritual wickedness in high places."

Do you know your adversary? Do you know how he works? You would be amazed yet horrified by the schemes that he conjures up to get you to lose your way.

I had a dream and a revelation of who the devil is, and how he works. I am not saying that this is the only way, but for us children of God, he is forever plotting to see how he can get us over to his side. Sometimes he comes as a roaring lion, then there are times that he comes as a wolf in sheep's clothing, and even other times when the devil presents himself as an angel of light - this is where most Christians are caught off guard. Unfortunately for some, they do not realize their predicament until it's too late. I probably shouldn't use the term "too late", for once there is life there is hope. Instead, I'll say that those who are deceived do not realize it until after they have missed out on so much that the Lord had for them.

I would like you to come with me on a journey and so I may give you insight on just how the devil works. I will share with you a dream that I had. I take dreams very seriously, as I believe it is God speaking to me, and I consider myself an interpreter of dreams.

Picture if you will a beautiful spring morning in May. You decide to go for an early morning walk. There is a slight breeze and the smell of various blossoming trees and flowers permeate the air like freshly washed laundry engulfed in fabric softener. Birds are chirping joyfully in the trees and squirrels chase each other along the branches. You are caught up in the beauty of nature, and as you bounce along, quietly humming the song "How Great Thou Art". All of a sudden, you feel like a pebble or something hit you in the back. You ignore it, thinking that it might've been an acorn that fell from an overhanging branch. But then you feel it again and this time you turn around to see a dark, robust man about seven feet tall approaching and grinning from ear to ear. As he gets closer you realize that he walks with a limp, and a putrid smell exudes from his body. Without an introduction, you immediately know who he is. You realize that what he was doing was throwing spitballs at you. (Substitute the p in spitball for an h) They were spitballs of debts, lies, sickness, tiredness and loss. It was difficult to tell his age, but he looked like he could be in his late 40s. His piercing charcoal black eyes appeared as if they were looking straight through you, and you got a sense that he had been around for quite some time.

He catches up to you and gets into step with you. The smell is so horrible that it takes all your willpower not to throw up. You realize that he has a sore foot that was apparently rotting away because it had not been taken care of. You figure he got that when God cast him out of heaven. You ask him why he threw those spitballs at you, but he denies it. Needless to say you knew he was lying and that it was him. You look him straight in the eyes and say, "Who Do You Think You Are? You slew foot, stinking, rotten devil! Get away from me, leave me alone, I know who you are, and I don't want anything to do with you." You start quoting scriptures at him: "The Lord is my light and my salvation whom shall I fear?" (Psalms 27:1) "Yea though I walk through the valley of the shadow of death, I shall fear no evil. Thy rod and thy staff they comfort me." (Psalms 23) "I am the resurrection and the life, he that believeth in me though he were dead yet shall he live and whosoever lives and believeth in me shall never die." (John 11:25, 26) You even quote lines from a song you heard your father say when he was having nightmares and thought there were evil spirits lurking around. "Jesus, the name high over all in hell or earth and sky, angels and men before it fall and devils fear and flee." ("Jesus, the Name High Over All") At the name of Jesus the devil has to flee, so that's just what he did!

After a little while you begin to feel tired and frustrated because it seems as if you are not reaching your destination and instead of walking straight down the road, you start walking from one side to the other. Spitballs of doubt, fear, loneliness and guilt start bombarding you from every side, and you can't see who is responsible for throwing them but they are coming at you fiercely with others like self-pity, envy, discouragement, greed, prayerlessness and pride. You start catching them and before long it seems like a game to you and you are taking great delight in seeing how many you could catch as if you are accomplishing some great feat. At times you see the devil in camouflage poking his head out from behind buildings, trees and even people as if you were playing hide and go seek with him and it does not seem to register with you that he is the one behind all your confusion.

You continue walking and meet Brother Mark from the church, and you exchange pleasantries, he asks you where you are off to and you tell him that you are going on a trip. He proceeds to ask you about your destination and the time of your flight, but you do not seem to know exactly where you are going. You tell him that you had a ticket in your pocket, but you do not bother to take it out and look. Having a confused look on his face, he takes the liberty to inform you that there is a store not too far away where you can purchase some clothes and other supplies for your trip. (He obviously saw that you were not prepared for your journey and wasn't walking right). You ignore what he is saying and continue to walk on.

As Brother Mark leaves, going in the opposite direction, he tries one last time calling out, "What time is your trip?"

"I don't know," you yell back, still unconcerned and showing a lack of interest in the details.

You continue walking down the road, and guess who shows up again? Yes, old Slew foot. This time he deliberately comes up close to you and starts a conversation. You are laughing and talking with him as if you were old friends, and somehow he does not seem as horrible and awful as when you first saw him. His smell does not seem to bother you anymore. He is hugging you and holding you close as you trudged along. He shares with you that he was married, but that his wife was dying. He asked you if you wanted to meet her and without any hesitation you say yes.

Before long you come to a one room box house that has only a window and no door. You look in and see the most dreadful sight that you have ever seen. There is a woman lying on the bare floor in filth. She is mere skin and bones, her hair a matted, stringy mess, and her sunken eyes seem to sink deeper as she gasps for breath. You think, *how sad.*

Hanging on a wooden frame over her is a portrait of a beautiful young lady and old slew foot answered your question before you could even ask it. "That is what she looked like when we first met," he says with a freakish grin on his face. You walk away and ask him why he had not taken care of her; he sidesteps the question and says instead that she still loves him, but he did not love her anymore. He goes on to tell you that she was going to die soon and that he will remarry. And who knows; you might very well be the next lucky bride. He says, "I could give you anything you want. You would not have to worry about anything again."

You hear what he says and even after what you witnessed, your heart seems to leap for joy and feel privileged to receive such an offer. You decide right then and there that you will accept his proposal should he ask. (Be aware, the devil comes to steal, kill and destroy. He is a liar from the pit of hell and he has no love or use for you but bring you down to nothing like the woman whose life he had messed up and was left with nothing but skin and bones.) You walk on thinking of life where you would not need anything and the great life that you would have being married to a powerful man that could take care of all your needs.

After a few miles of daydreaming you arrive at a bus stop where you are greeted by a sister from your church. She is your good friend and you get to talking. After a short time you could see the bus approaching. The bus stops and folks are in line to get on the bus and your friend asks if you already have a ticket. You reply yes, but then you proceed to look for change to get on the bus. Your sister friend begins helping you look for change to get on the bus until eventually the last person gets on the bus and it pulls away. You both started running after the bus and yelling, "Stop, wait for us," but it was too late. You felt like because you were at the bus stop that there was no way the bus should have left without you.

How could I explain this to you? You could be in the house, but still lost. As someone puts it, "Sitting in the garage does not make you a car." You allowed the enemy to overwhelm you with the issues of life and at some point you lost your way. We have to know how the enemy works and that he will use whoever, whenever and whatever he could to deter you from your goal. Don't get caught up in schemes of the devil where you don't know whether you are coming or going.

You were both left behind because you were not ready period. Don't allow anyone to make you lose your way. Some people you just can't help. You've encouraged and advised and have given your all, and it gets to the point that you just have to break those ties and just put them on the alter before God. Don't let anyone make you miss out on heaven.

As you stand there dazed and confused, you put your hands in your pockets, and it comes into contact with your ticket. You pull it out of your pocket and examine it. You found out that you had a 9:30 flight that same morning, right about the time that you had met your church brother. It is now 4:30 in the afternoon. You realize that not only had you missed your flight, but you had also caused someone else to miss out also. Heed the warning! Someone might have been telling you to make it right with the Lord and you may have brushed them off because you are young and you think that serving God is for old people and you have to enjoy your youth, but one never knows what the next day holds and it is not promised to us so I will encourage you to "seek him while he could be found." (Isaiah 55:6) The best decision that you can make in life is to give God your life.

~~~

The best decision that you can make in life is to give God your life

~~~

Chapter 17

I MUST DECREASE SO THAT HE WILL INCREASE

My God, here I am thinking about that time tomorrow. That time that I have come to dread. That time when the pastor says, "As the ministers come to pray for those who need prayer." You may ask why I dread it and what caused me to be so fearful or dread that particular time? Well, here it is.

I walk up and I stand in the front of the church with all the other ministers. I see people come up for prayer, they pass me by and move on to someone else. It is even worse if I happen to be standing beside the pastor's wife. There would be a long line waiting for her to pray for them, and in a way I understand that reasoning; no hard feelings or anything, she is a great and powerful woman of God. But in the meantime, my heart is breaking into tiny pieces. I stand there feeling ignored, feeling unappreciated, and more or less feeling useless and worthless.

At first, I encourage myself, and think, "If you only knew who it was that wanted to pray for you, you would be running and knocking me over in anticipation." I think of Jesus with the woman at the well, how he asked for a drink of water, then he said to her, "If thou knewest the gift of God, and who it is that saith to thee, Give me to drink; thou wouldest have asked of him, and he would have given thee living water". (John 4:10)

It is like going to the bank to cash a small check, and a certain man comes up to you and ask you for some money, maybe $20, and you look at him thinking, *Why are you asking me for money, I hardly have enough of myself?!* But later you find out that the man was Bill Gates. You realize that he really did not need your $20, but he just wanted to see your reaction, test your faith, and see the true person that you are when placed in a particular situation. Did you give him the $20 or did you say, "Go about your business and leave me alone!"? That is how I feel when I am standing up there to pray for people, and they ignore me and pass me by.

I think to myself, *I have seen God answer my prayers so many times and in so many ways, and in so many situations, they just don't know what they are missing.* I start questioning myself. *Is it because they don't know me, do I not look the part, is it because I have an accent....* and the list goes on. And it hurts.

A few times individuals come to me to pray with them, and I feel so grateful. Then there were times as I stood up there and my son or my daughter came to me to pray for them. I wondered if they came solely because they felt sorry for me. I asked later, and they each said no, that was not the case... but still I wondered.

I often asked myself and God what was going on because it seemed as if I was always in a situation where I got passed over, was underappreciated, made to feel inferior, and looked down on, and He finally showed it to me!

He showed me that I was being prepared to be in a position where I would be on the other end, where folks would be looking up to me that are going to be in the same situation that I am in right now, and it was for me to be a lifeline so to speak. I was to be someone who did not judge them by their looks, how they dressed, or their social status, but would see their souls as God sees them.

There is too much partiality in the church. God is looking for His people who will love as He loves, will care for one another as He cares for us as stated in John 13:35. "By this shall they know that ye are my disciples if ye have love one towards another". This is the way that the world will recognize us as Christians. We don't have to go around in long dresses, having religious bumper stickers on the car, or carrying around a big Bible so that all can see. No!

We should not find pleasure in humiliating and degrading others less privileged than ourselves. Instead, we should build one another up. Let us examine ourselves and see where we stand.

God is taking me through this learning process and it hurts. But just as He is working with me, I know He is going to help you. He is going to maneuver you through the process of learning, and you will learn to seek Him, and as you to do, you will come to understand what He is requiring of you in this season and what His will is for your life. Do not be despondent. God will not give you more than you can handle. It may seem near impossible to get through the tests, but this process is necessary. How else will you be able to relate to the people God has strategically sent your way? If it's all peaches and cream, there is no opportunity to pour out your soul to God. Why would you have to exercise faith and learn to depend on Him completely? How would you know what it feels like to just have bread and water? My God!

We have to learn how to love the poor and less fortunate the same way that we love those who are rich and have everything going for them.

I see the separation and meanness happening all the time. At my former church where there were just a handful of people, I barely got asked to preach, but on this particular Sunday I was teaching Sunday school and the Holy Spirit moved on me in such a way that it was no more teaching but preaching. I felt boldness like I never had before. I was preaching on the subject "The Water That Is In You Shall Be A Well of Water Springing Up Into Everlasting Life". The whole church was on fire! When it came time for the pastor to preach, he could not preach the message that he had prepared, he had to go back to my message. You would think that he would be happy or even proud of me, but oh no, what he said to me when church was over was, "Next time leave the preaching to me". Not too long after that I was no longer Sunday School Superintendent. I was overlooked and compartmentalized, placed in a box as so many Christians are today, and not allowed to explore their full potential.

People who have come after me have misused opportunities for mutual fellowship and mentorship. Some have done so because of elitism, and it left me out in the cold.

I used to ask myself why I was iced out. Was it because I was not American born and raised? Was it because I was overweight? What did they see when they looked at me?

Was it because they didn't know me? Was it because I didn't have anyone to validate me?

The last question struck me and I finally stopped turning around in circles. You know why? I realized I didn't need anyone to validate me. If God gave me His stamp of approval, that's everything I need! Everyone else will follow and will submit and will be subject to Him based on Romans 8:31: "What shall we say then to these things? If God be for us, who can be against us?"

Yes, yes, yes! I was having a pity party, but I learned something at church that Sunday that changed my way of thinking. You see, I had gone to church with a made up mind that whether or not someone came to me for prayer, I would hold my head up high and give God thanks. As the word went forth, I was further encouraged. As the pastor preached on the topic "How To Be A Better Friend", I knew it was God talking. The text was taken from John 1:20. He used John the Baptist as an example. He said, "John the Baptist empathetically stated that he was not the Christ, but was only a conduit for the one that was to follow Jesus Christ, the son of God". He went on to say that John was in no way, shape, or form intimidated by Jesus coming on the scene. He used these most profound words: "I must decrease, so that he will increase". (John 3:30)

On that particular Sunday, I realized that the lesson I was supposed to learn in that season of my life was that I am not the Christ! It is not about me, it is all about him. I made up my mind to decrease, so that he would increase. I determined that if it meant being stepped on and over, having to go through humiliation, so be it! By God's grace I would be strong and fight the good fight of faith. I determined that I would "run this race with patience, looking unto Jesus the author and finisher of my faith". (Hebrews 12:1-2)

In John 3:26-29 some of John's disciples, and also some of Jesus' disciples, were quick to report to John that Jesus was also baptizing. (That was not entirely correct - Jesus himself wasn't actually doing the baptizing, it was his disciples.) Everybody was going to him to be baptized. Those making the report were probably trying to cause strife between John and Jesus, trying to make it a competition – just as you find in many churches today. But John did not get frustrated or perturbed in the least. In fact, he reminded "the reporters" that he was just a friend of the bridegroom, and because he was a true friend, he was happy for the bridegroom: honored, yet grateful, to be serving in the capacity that was assigned to him.

John was also Jesus' cousin, and even though he was older, he knew his role. John was not jealous, he did not have a chip on his shoulder, and he faithfully completed his assignment against all odds and in his own way. He dressed different, he looked different, his diet was different even where he chose to serve (in the desert) was different.

This brings me to a very important point. It is okay to be different. Many Christians today feel they need to fit in. Jesus did not fit in. In fact, he did things differently. He talked differently. In John 7:46 it states that "never man spake like this man". You may do things differently, you may talk differently, such as with an accent, and you may dress differently. Different makes you stand out, and sometimes not in a positive way. But once you are doing

76

what thus saith the Lord, you need not fear. You will be talked about, you will be criticized, you might even be ignored, but you just go right on fighting that good fight of faith.

You find many Christians in churches today are robotic Christians. They move the same, they speak the same, and they dance the same – it's like they were programmed like the 2004 movie "The Stepford Wives"! This movie was based on the 1972 novel where the wives were practically perfect. Cooked the perfect meal, kept the perfect house, had the perfect shape, dressed perfectly; they were all basically the same, and the reader later realized that they were not real, they were androids.

God made each and every one of us different. No two people are alike. We all are given different gifts and talents, and we have to walk in our calling. You would think that in the church you are free from discrimination and prejudices, but that is not the case. When Jesus was on earth, it was the religious rulers and leaders that brought accusations against him and even plotted to kill him. Jesus later stated that "all that will live godly in Christ Jesus shall suffer persecution". (2 Timothy 3:12) These robotic Christians are mentioned in 2 Timothy 3:5 "having a form of godliness, but denying the power thereof". These Christians go through the motions, they say the right things, but underneath it all, there is no power, no sincerity, and no love. May God help us all!

If you find yourself in this predicament, of being a Stepford Christian, ask God to make you over again. Pray: "Lord, renew a right spirit within me."

Let us be propelled by the Holy Spirit and not by man-made stimulants. This may sound tough, but I'm just keeping it real. The truth must be told. We throw around the phrase "on one accord", but we have to realize that being on one accord is to be led by the spirit of God, and flowing together in the spirit. It is not doing "church" as usual. It is not just going through the motions.

I must warn you that I will be transparent; some might even think that I am being too transparent, but I have to keep it real, or else it's not worth it. I tend to think like my daddy: he wants it all. He desires total surrender and for us to serve him with our whole heart; ninety nine and a half is not good enough. He wants all of us; my kids always laugh at me and say, "There she goes, miss all or nothing." I tell you, there is someone else who also wants all of you, and that is the main reason why you have to fight this good fight of faith. "Satan's desire is to have you and to sift you as wheat". (Luke 22:31) He wants it all also. He will not stop trying, he does not give up because his goal is not only to "steal, but to kill and ultimately to destroy". (John 10:10)

If you know that is someone's intention where you are concerned, won't you be prepared to fight with all your might? Then what are you waiting for? We must follow Nehemiah's example when he was threatened by Sanballat and Tobiah as he was rebuilding the walls of Jerusalem. Get your "swords, spears and bows... Don't be afraid, remember the Lord who is great and awesome, and fight for your families, your sons and your daughters, your wives and your homes". (Nehemiah 4:13-14)

Chapter 18

DENYING SELF

Denying self... This is a difficult concept.

What does it really mean to deny self? Does it mean that you deny yourself of earthly goods, live like a pauper, wear clothing that is not too flashy, drive an inexpensive car, or overall live a simple mundane life?

No, definitely not so.

To deny self is to give up something or someone (usually temporarily) in order for God to work in and through you. Denying self is to make a sacrifice to give up something that you enjoy, usually something that takes up a lot of your time may not be categorized as sin, but one sometimes has to give them up, in order to spend more time with God, and to seek His face. It could be as simple as turning off the music in your car and speaking to Jesus instead. It could be giving up a meal and dedicating that time to praying and reading your Bible. It could be getting out of your bed an hour earlier, when what you really feel like doing is cuddling that warm blanket and pillow, and getting as much sleep as you possibly could.

I venture to say that in the Christian community that one of the main reasons we don't see our dreams fulfilled, don't reach a place where we want to go, is that we refuse to deny self.

Denying self is a conscious decision that one has to make. It is not an easy task because it is basically going against what the flesh desires.

The first step in the race to deny self is to acknowledge that we are more of a spiritual being that is just renting this natural body of flesh covering. We, therefore, have to live in the spirit. In order to do that, we have to connect spiritually with the Almighty, realizing that we cannot do much in our own strength, but that all our help comes from the Lord. We have to walk in the spirit, talk in the spirit, sing in the spirit and live in the spirit.

You might be thinking, *Well, how do I accomplish this feat?* First, you start your day off right. You wake up in the morning and you thank the Lord for the beautiful day that He has made, and make a conscious decision that you will "rejoice and be glad in it" (Psalm 118:24). You will spend some quality time with God which will include worship, prayer and Bible reading. Allow Him to direct your path and ask Him to make you a blessing to everyone you encounter. Ask God to have control of your mouth, eyes, hands and feet, to basically be a Christ-led robot.

Is there an assignment that you know for sure that He has given you? Whether it is to give up something or someone, read your Bible in the morning instead of at night when your eyes are closing and you can't seem to stay awake, give up the bad habits such as the cigarettes that you use to calm you, let Him be your peace! The alcohol that you run to in order to deal with your problems, the illicit sex that you feel you need to feel loved, the food you run to for comfort, let Jesus be those things to you.

Trust me, all you need may be found in Jesus. He knows what you are going through and all the hurt and pain that you may be experiencing. He wants you to know that if you "trust in the Lord with all [your] heart and lean not to your own understanding, but in all [your] ways acknowledge him, that he will direct your path." (Proverbs 3:5-6)

What has God asked you to give up that you are still holding onto? You see, God wants to take you to higher heights and deeper depths, and He wants you to reach your destiny, but given the condition that you are in right now, you will not be able to go all the way. There are things that need to be worked on and out so that they may come into alignment. It is like a car: you are going on a long journey so you need an oil change; you need to check the brakes, the tires, see if you need more than a tune-up, and make sure the filters are clean and the car is in good working condition, so that it does not break down on the trip. God is trying to prepare us and tune us up for our journey, making sure that we are clean and ready, but it is up to us to yield to His will and His way. We need to get rid of the weight that is preventing us from going forward, and the sooner we do what He desires of us, it is that much faster that we will realize the great things that He has in store for us.

Sometimes we wonder why we have not received those things that God has promised us. Well, let me tell you, the problem is not with God. It is with us. We are waiting on God while God is waiting on us to do what He asked us to do for such a long time, back to "God knows when". The place God is taking us requires discipline, steadfastness and total dependence on Him. We have to get ourselves on a routine of self-denial and seeking God's face, not His hand. Ask not what can you do for me God; instead ask what He would have you do?

We are being called to a place where we will have to intercede for the sick even when we are not well ourselves. We are going to be called upon to encourage others when we ourselves are going through and need encouragement. We need to come to that place where we can smile while all hell is breaking lose in our lives. "We walk by faith and not by sight" (2 Corinthians 5:7) and "we call those things that are not as though they were." (Romans 4:17).

Just think: do you want to be hired for your dream job only to realize a few months later that you were not prepared for what it entails, and you end up getting fired or undergoing a nervous breakdown? God is getting us ready and the test and trials that we are going through might seem tough and unbearable, and we may wonder why we have to go through these things anyway, but the end result will be so great that we might even ask ourselves why it took us so long to straighten up.

God needs to know that He can trust us, and that we will be faithful through thick and thin. You see, the flesh desires to have control of our lives, and it has to be crucified in order for the spirit to reign supreme. There is a fight going on every second between the flesh and the spirit; that's why we find ourselves doing things that we don't want to do like eating those cookies that we swear we wouldn't eat and neglecting things we need to do like reading the Bible.

Have you ever decided to go on a fast and all of a sudden you have people offering you food to eat who you don't even know? You smell food that doesn't even exist, you feel you want to eat healthy all of a sudden. Oh that salad looks so good, when you don't even like salad. You are tempted to eat things you don't even care for, and you wake up with a headache, and feel dizzy like you're going to pass out, faint away, and even die all because you decided to fast and deny self.

Has someone ever done you wrong and all you want to do is get back at them, your flesh craving revenge and retribution? But then the spirit of the Lord tells you that He will fight your battles for you. You are prompted to be nice to the person, even to the point where you end up serving him/her? That is what it means to deny self.

Yolanda Adams sang "is your all on the altar of sacrifice laid, your heart doth the spirit control, you can only be blessed and have peace and sweet rest, as you yield Him your body and soul." To deny self is to spiritually die to the flesh. It is not a one-time thing; it is something that we must do daily. We at times get so caught up in ourselves, so much so as to think that we have arrived and have conquered the flesh, only to get a rude awakening. This old flesh will try to rise to the top like a bag of air.

I had a relationship with this person in the church. I knew it wasn't going anywhere, but I liked the attention. Anyway, this particular day I went to this person's house to deliver a message. I felt strong, I was walking in the spirit, I felt that I had overcome the flesh and all that was behind me. As soon as I stepped to the door and he appeared, that old flesh just seemed to rise up in me from God only knows where. The gentleman was obviously home alone, and I knew that he was feeling what I was feeling. We spoke at the door for some time, and then he asked me to come in. I quickly refused and I knew if I had stepped into that house that there would be no turning back. I proceeded to say bye and ran to my car so fast, so discombobulated that I found myself in the passenger seat instead of the driver seat. I was that shaken up. I must have been saying in my mind, "Jesus take the wheel". I felt silly and humiliated as I walked around to the other side, with him looking at me from the doorway. I drove off as best as I could, and on the highway I called him said, "I really had to get out of there quickly." He said something that I really did not expect him to say. He said, "Why don't you come back?" I was like, "What on earth?!"

I learned something that day: it does not matter how spiritual you might be feeling, you cannot let your guard down. You have to keep your antenna up and on the alert, and take heed that when you think you're standing so strong and tall, you'll fall. (1 Corinthians 10:12)

Your experience is not everyone's experience, and you should not expect others to act and do what you think they should do, even if they are in the church, have been saved longer than you and/or hold a higher position than you do. There are Christians who claim to be saved, sanctified, and filled with the blessed Holy Ghost, but still the flesh is not crucified in their lives.

In Galatians 2:20 Paul clearly states, "I am crucified with Christ: nevertheless I live; yet not I, but Christ liveth in me." Like Paul, we have to come to that place where we realize that it is not by our own strength that the flesh could be crucified, but by the power of God that lives within us. Paul was willing to die for the gospel of Jesus Christ. It was even from the early part of his conversion where Ananias conversed with him, that Paul was told that he had to suffer for Christ. This did not deter him, but instead he considered it an honor to be able to suffer for his sake.

Although the Lord lives in us, He has given us free will. He does not force Himself on us. God shows us what we should do through the Holy Spirit and the word of God. Yet ultimately we have to make that choice for ourselves. Just like a parent teaches her child to do certain things, but the child eventually does what he or she chooses to do.

We have to consider ourselves dead to sin, but alive in the spirit. "Except a corn of wheat fall into the ground and die, it abideth alone: but if it die, it bringeth forth much fruit." (John 12:24) In order for us to live to our full potential, we have to first die to flesh and self. We wonder at times why we don't see the fruit of our labor, well guess what? We haven't died yet. That's it, right there in a nutshell. Maybe that's why some of us ladies are still not married. We are afraid to die. "Oh, I need my independence, nobody can tell me what to do, I don't feel I have to submit to my husband. There shouldn't be any head or tail, we should be equal." With that kind of attitude, we don't need to get married because God does not bless our mess.

God is trying to take us to that place that He has promised, but first we must go through a process, and like the seed, we must die. We must go through that dark place in our lives where we seem to be all alone, where the sun does not seem to be shining, where all around us is dirt, we are walked on, we are dumped on, but we know that He has promised that He will never leave us nor forsake us. (Deuteronomy 31:6)

The light of God's love is still shining on us even when it doesn't feel or look like it. He is cleansing us by the washing of water, which is the Word, and we have been plowed by the oxygen, which is the Holy Spirit. That is all that we as the seed need to grow. Sunshine, water and air. Before you know it, we have risen with Him, we start growing, we start to poke through the dirt, we continue to grow and blossom, and eventually we bring forth fruit which will encourage, feed and strengthen others. Blessed be the name of the Lord! That's what it means when it says in John 4:14, "he shall be in [you] a well of water, springing up into everlasting life." Like a spring or a fountain and even a waterfall, the water comes from deep within and flows over so that those who are around or come close will get wet, will experience some of what you have, and in turn will tell others. Those others will not just come to you, but to the source of the fountain. That fountain, according to hymnodist William Cowper, is filled with blood. He writes, "There is a fountain filled with blood. Drawn from Immanuel's veins; and sinners plunged beneath that flood, Lose all their guilty stains." Thanks be to God!

Chapter 19

LIVETH:
Living In Victory Even Through Hardship

One songwriter penned these words:

"Good things don't come easy, it took all my prayer meetings and all my praying and fasting, good things don't come easy."

I don't know about you, but for me, I've had to fight hard for everything that I have. I had to fight to be in America. I worked over six years to get my papers filed for my residence. I've had to fight to feed my kids, fight to keep a roof over our heads, fight to pay the mortgage, fight to keep my head above water, fight not to be overlooked, and fight to keep my sanity. You name it, I've had to fight for it.

Life is a continuous fight, and regardless of how long you've been in the fight, you still have to continue fighting. Why? Because if you stop, you are giving up and you will lose the fight.

I am reminded of movies that I have seen which involve boxing. We have a contestant who gets beaten to a blooded pulp, and you think that it's all over and that there's no more fight left in him. Yet somehow his strength seems to be renewed and the boxer comes back fiercer than ever. Maybe it's a picture in his mind of his kids not having food, his wife leaving, or even a person who told him he couldn't do it. He musters up some remnant of strength, and he gives it all his strength and he wins! That is how it should be with us as Christians: we realize that our strength does not lie within our means - God is our strength.

We need to be reminded at times of who is fighting our battles. Look back at the victories He has won for us. Embrace that memory and keep it moving, i.e., keep on fighting.

Fight for Our Children

We have to fight for our children. We have to realize that God gave us the responsibility of taking care of them, and it is our duty to bring them up in the fear and admonition of the Lord. Even when we tell them the same thing over and over again, and they don't seem to hear or care, we must continue to point them in the right direction. Eventually the light bulb will turn on in their heads and they will finally get the picture of what we have been trying to show them all along.

Fight for Our Destiny

We must fight for destiny. Someone said that many of us will be disappointed when we get to heaven, although technically, there is no disappointment in heaven. But what the speaker was trying to convey is that when we get to heaven and God shows us all that He had for us down on earth, we may want to kick ourselves because we didn't have enough faith or failed to go that extra mile to receive all the blessings here.

In 2004, the Lord told me as I was taking a shower that I was not going to get married until I lost the weight. Now do I want to get married? Yes. Do I believe God spoke to me? Yes. Have I lost the weight? No. In fact, I seem to be gaining more weight with every year that goes by. There it is, another fight! The battle of the bulge! I have tried many diets, but failed. I've bought many exercise machines and pieces of equipment, but have not used them. I've joined several gyms, have paid the monthly fees, but failed to even go to the gym. I eat whatever I like, even though I know it is full of fat and calories which are not good for me. And here it is 2018, and I haven't lost the weight and am not remarried.

At times I get frustrated that I am by myself with no one to talk to, paying all the bills by myself, working overtime to make ends meet, and having no one to support me with the kids... but who is to blame for that? NO ONE BUT ME.

I'll take it a step further. The Lord showed me in a dream what I had to do to lose the weight. He put me on a LIVETH, not a diet. But what did I do? I complained that it is too tough. I wanted to substitute this for that and alter His instructions. When I got fed up with my lack of progress, I started following God's instructions to the T, and guess what? I lost the weight, felt and looked great, and I said to the Lord, "Lord, I lost the weight, but I don't see the husband." I wanted a husband right away, and was disappointed when it did not happen. So I retreated to my old lifestyle.

I later asked God, "Why didn't you send my husband? I did what you said." He answered me, "Look at yourself now." That is when I realized what God was trying to show me. He wanted me to know that my desires for weight loss, companionship, and support would not *be* addressed by a quick fix. I needed to make a change in my routine which involves exercise and a healthy eating lifestyle. God wanted me to eat right and to refuse to allow the physical need for food to take priority over the spiritual food. He wanted us to spend more time together. I've learned that I can't just please God today because I want something from Him; I must please him every day – every single day.

I remember when I was a teenager if I wanted some money or to go somewhere, I cleaned the whole house until it was spotless, washed the clothes, did the dishes, or whatever else my parents asked me to do to make extra money or earn the privilege of going. I wanted to make sure that there was nothing that they could look to deny me. I was ready, I was prepared, but that was just for that day, because I needed something from my parents in the moment. Truly I knew what their response would be if there was work to be done, so I cleared the work off the bench so to speak to remove all objections to my request. Back then I thought I was so smart, and that I had gotten something over on them, but they knew what I was doing, yet they chose to give me my desires anyway.

God is not like man. He sees way down to the end of the road, in fact He knows our end even before our beginning. God knows that if He gives us certain things before we are ready for them, down the road it will all fall apart and cause us more heartache and the pain than what we might be going through at the present time. Also, many lives would be affected in a negative way. To avoid all that God withholds good from us until we are ready to receive,

90

appreciate, cherish and keep that which he gives to us. To receive those good things, we must change our lifestyle.

I believe that God is calling us to a place of greater intimacy with Him, and to accomplish that we need to be willing to make some sacrifices. God is calling for some of us to fast daily; spend quality time with Him in prayer and Bible study, praise, and worship; and to spend some quiet time in meditation where we could listen to what He is saying to us.

I was asked this question by one of the sisters in church after teaching on Philip's experience in Acts 8:39-40, where he was transported to another place. "Why don't we experience such great miracles such as: being transported, the dead brought back to life, the blind seeing and the lame walking?" I firmly believe that the key to unlock those doors lie in our relationship with God. We must be willing to make the kind of sacrifice that entails going out on a limb. This simply means that while others are feasting, we are fasting. While others are sleeping, we are seeking. While others are partying, we are praying. While others are resting, we are reading. When others are sighing, we are singing. And when others are dating, we are waiting.

Are we ready to be a pastor's wife if we can't pray for one hour, if we don't know how to intercede to God on behalf of our husband and the church?

We are not ready to counsel members if our tongues are forked like a serpents, and we don't know how to love and forgive.

I am not ready to be anyone's wife if I don't know how to cook healthy meals.

I want to take care of my husband in every way: the bedroom, the bathroom, the living room and the kitchen. Spiritually, mentally, physically, and emotionally. To do so, I have to be willing to sacrifice.

People are going to come over to your house, sometimes unexpectedly, and you should be able to entertain them – offer a sandwich, slice of cake, and something to drink. If it is lunch time or dinner time, be prepared and ready to invite them to join you. Call me "old school", but back home if we were preparing a meal and someone passed by, we would automatically get out another plate or bowl, regardless of how meager the meal may have seemed. (Yes, even though sometimes it was just chicken backs and necks.)

Some of you would have no idea what I'm talking about, but I have learned to ask God's blessing on the last meal in the house, not knowing where the next one would be coming from. The kids would eat it and enjoy it even asking if there was more. I'm talking about macaroni and cheese without milk or maybe even butter because there was none. Mashed potatoes without milk and chicken gizzards. Thank you Jesus!

When I remember those times, I have to take a praise break. Hallelujah! I sing praises to His name and join with the singer Mr. Andrae Crouch in his song "My Tribute" when he says "how can I say thanks for all the things He's done for me".

Do you understand now why God does not give us certain things when we think we should have them? Do you understand that to get to our destiny that we have to give up some stuff and make some sacrifices?

We have to fight the good fight of faith, wondering about where we could have been if only we were willing to exercise our faith and do those things that God has called us to do? As I said, it is a daily fight.

My battle is with my weight. I am determined now that I am going to go on my "liveth process plan" (Living In Victory Even Through Hardship). Whatever your battle, ask God to direct your faith to fit the process you are going through. Your hardship may be dealing with a husband who is abusive, maybe an illness that renders you helpless at times where you have to depend on others for your daily care. It might even be the challenge of finding the money to pay the bills every month. But regardless of what that hardship is, you could live in victory. No matter what it is, keep on fighting that good fight of faith knowing that the battle really is not yours but the Lord's.

Ladies, for those of you who are single and think that they are ready to get married I want to ask you to do a little soul searching and ask yourself these few questions. "Do I really want to get married when I'm not comfortable with my body? How could I expect my husband to be comfortable with my body if I'm not comfortable with it? Am I ready for marriage when I don't love and respect myself? How then can I expect my husband to love and respect me? Am I waiting for a husband to complete me? I'll tell you right now, he can't complete you, only God can. Am I ready for marriage if I am selfish, if it's all about me and what I want and need? Is it always my way or the highway? Marriage is a give and take and in order for it to work, both sides have to be willing to make sacrifices. Men this goes for you also. You have to be willing to step up to the plate and do your duty as a provider and a protector. We see so many broken homes because men neglect their roles in the family and the women have to step up and take charge. I do not believe that women want to wear the pants but sometimes they are left with no other choice.

Ladies, the both of you are in this together, but you have to learn as a wife that the more you love him, the more he will love you. You can't go wrong. If he doesn't love you in return, he's just heaping coals of fire on his head. You have to do your part without murmuring or complaining; do everything in love.

I see marriage as becoming one as God said, so if I see my husband bleeding, I am going to do all in my power to stop that bleed because in reality I am also bleeding. If my husband makes sure that he treats me well, maybe saying, "Go treat yourself to a new wardrobe honey, get your hair done", that is one way to know he appreciates me and the sacrifices I make, or even a simple thing like helping with the dishes. When I walk beside my husband, I want him to be proud of me, and vice a versa.

I don't understand, especially in the church, how a speaker or minister fails to acknowledge his or her significant other. Are they ashamed? What kind of marriage do they have? It perplexes me when I never see them holding hands, hugging, or smiling at each other; they never show any kind of affection toward one another. I don't know how they ride in the car: I imagine you could cut the atmosphere with a knife for how thick it is.

Marriage should be enjoyed, not endured. If we love our spouse as God loved us, we would not be in the predicament that we are in today with people not wanting to get married. People are scared to get married because they fear that it will end in divorce. Couples want to live together first to see how they get along, and some prefer to just "shack up" indefinitely so that there is no commitment. If it does not work out they go their separate ways. If Christian who are the light of the world would shine in their marriages as they should; love, care and respect each other as they should; then there would not be so many divorces and life overall would be more healthy and happy.

My God, when I was explaining about my LIVETH plan, I did not know that a few days later that I would have to live what I preached.

As a single parent with no family around, at times I find that I can't always make the little money that I have stretch. I am private a person and don't want to tell anyone about my situation. Sometimes I don't have money for groceries, gas, or to pay the bills that are due. I do not feel comfortable saying anything to anyone. You may ask why I don't ask my friends in the church or on the job, but what it all boils down to that I cannot allow myself to be that vulnerable. Do you know what I am talking about? I believe people love and care about me, but I don't feel close enough to anyone to tell them these things. Some people prey on your vulnerability, and welcome the opportunity to see you struggle and are ecstatic when you are forced to come to them for help. That's not the way it should be, but I'm just telling you how it is with me.

I always run to God, and either He supplies my needs or He gives me the grace to endure until I can do better. As I am writing this passage, I am going through this situation and would like share it as a great example of liveth.

My electric bill is overdue. I thought I had a week before they took action, so I had purposed in my heart that when I got paid the following Friday that I would take care of it. I came home from work on Friday and my older son met me outside the garage to inform me that the electricity had been shut off. It was the month of August and in Atlanta it is warm. Thank God I was not in a cold climate! I thought to myself, *the neighbors must have seen the truck come by, and I thank God that I was not home.* Talk about humiliation! Seeing that we had no electricity, my older son decided that he would spend a few days with a cousin. He is 21; what kind of life would he have if he could not charge his cell phone, go on the computer, be able to watch television, or use any electronic devises? I felt like I had let him down and that I had somehow failed. Anyway, as he was going, I asked him to take an assortment of frozen meat to keep in our cousin's freezer until we could get the power back on. I was feeling somewhat under the weather, but realized that I had a gas stove and lots of food that I had to get rid of quick, fast and in a hurry... So I started cooking up a storm.

That evening, my younger son and I sat down at the table to a candlelight dinner. I thought to myself, "Some lady out there is wishing for a candlelight dinner and here I am in Lo-debar. (Lo-debar was a town mentioned in the

Old Testament in Gilead, referenced in 2 Samuel 9:4-5.) Lo-debar was considered a ghetto place, a place of lack and barrenness; that's where I found myself. But I knew that if I changed my attitude, I could change my circumstances.

So I got up, got two wine glasses, and pored us some grape juice to toast to the numerous blessings that were bestowed on us. We continued to enjoy the ambiance and basked in gratitude.

We must learn to be grateful and thankful for the things that we do have for there are others who are much worse off than we ever will be. Our families are healthy and well and that alone is enough to give God thanks for and to have an attitude of gratitude.

Through it all I am still fighting that good fight of faith. I have faith that someday I will not have to worry about money, how I am going to pay my bills, but that I will have more than enough so that I can help others in need. My desire is that people won't have to come and ask me, but that God will show me the needs in their lives and how I can be of help to them.

If you are out there going through hard and trying times, please keep the faith, for God is in control and He will come through for you in time. You may be married and your spouse cheated on you, and you feel as if you can't go on because your world has fallen apart. I am here to tell you, "Yes you can!" Hold your head up high and gather strength from the Lord. Are you grieving over someone who died? Life doesn't seem to have any meaning anymore? You don't want to get up in the morning and you feel you have nothing to live for? I want to let you know that there is a light at the end of the tunnel. God can grant peace to the troubled soul, He can cheer the fainting and calm the storms in your life. God knows your situation and He is working on your behalf even at this moment. There comes a time in your life when you have a choice whether to fight or to flee. Choose to fight. It is not a fad, it's for your FAD: you're fighting for your Family, your Anointing and for your Destiny!

Chapter 20

STAY TUNED UP AND FIT

Check this out.

When a person enlists in the US Armed Forces - be it Army, Navy, or Air Force - they have to go through some vigorous training or boot camp. They learn endurance and stamina, and build muscle and increase strength, and learn how to persevere. They experience hunger, thirst, tolerate extreme heat and cold, crawl through mud and possibly a swamp, and learn the art of camouflage.

These soldiers have to be fit and ready to combat the forces of the enemy when they come against them. They must have their gear ready at all times so even if they are called in the middle of the night, they are ready. The uniforms must be pressed and shoes polished and shining, with weapons cleaned and ready. You might wonder as I did why all this preparation, particularly the clothes, when the troops might have to crawl through mud. But then it was revealed to me that it's about who you represent. You can't just get up and go in clothes that you have been sleeping in or on, uniform all dirty and appearance haggard and unkempt, and expect anyone to take you seriously.

Showing up like that would make it appear as if you don't have any standards to adhere to, anything goes, and you would accept anything. Well, that is not the case. The

United States prides itself in training soldiers that are well groomed and prepared for the task that lies ahead. If these soldiers have to go through such grueling rituals on a daily basis, how much more we as children of the Most High God, Our Father who is the King of Kings and the Lord of Lords require of us!

We have to prepare ourselves on a daily basis. We have to "go through storms and rain, heartache and pain" as Marvin Sapp says in "My Testimony", and in order to do so successfully, we have to stay tuned up and fit. Trust me I know what I am talking about. I have put on quite a few pounds and instead of taking the shuttle to my job in the morning, I try to walk a mile or two to combat the pounds. I had gotten to the point where in climbing a little hill I would get short of breath and it felt like my heart was going to pop out of my chest! I looked and felt like I'd just run a marathon with sweat pouring out of every pore. Needless to say, I was not fit. What I realized though as I continued to walk it got easier and easier. When I got to the top of that hill, I figured that if I climbed it again and again, eventually it would be no problem. So I did it again, and soon it wasn't. You see, the hill did not change - I did.

We are admonished in Hebrews 12:1 to "lay aside the weight and the sin that doth so easily beset us." The weight is sin.

You must rid yourself of the weight and get ready for the battle to come. How do you get ready? Pray and read your Bible every day. Spend quality time with God. Walk and live in the Spirit. Say and do work pleasing to God. Live in a way that proclaims to the world that Lord is the head of your life. Now you are prepared for where He wants to take you! Now you are able to keep up.

Someone is waiting for you at the top of the hill. Are you going to sit at the bottom of it trying to catch your breath, or are you going to work at getting yourself together so you can charge that hill with zest?

I would like to encourage you to take it one day at a time. Isaiah 40:31 shares that "they that wait upon the Lord shall renew their strength." This waiting is not to stay in one place or to stand still, but to "keep moving" until you see what you are praying and trusting God for.

"They shall run and not be weary." (Isaiah 40:31) Now that you are doing – living in accord with God's will - on a daily basis, it is part of you. It's only natural to give God thanks when your eyes open in the morning and as you fall asleep at night. Don't get weary doing well, keep pushing. Do you get tired of being healthy? Of course not.

"They shall walk and not faint." (Isaiah 40:31) Even if it feels like 100° in your life, nothing seems to be going right, the bills are not paid, there's no money for food, the children are out of control, there's trouble on the job, friends are talking about you, your family is tired of you, or you're having health problems; don't worry, you will not faint. The Lord promised to renew your strength.

When someone faints as they are running a race, it is often because they get dehydrated. Don't allow that to happen to you. Get revived, cleansed and hydrated by the "washing of water by the word". Ephesians 5:26 The water is free. When it is offered you, take it and drink it, and pour it over your head if you must. You can't have too much of that water. Let the water be in you like a fountain springing up into everlasting life.

I must add this: do not be a fragile Christian who faints away with a little bad news, like those society ladies you see in the movies that's always swooning because all they do is go to dinners and brunch and gossip. They enjoy being lazy so they have no resistance whatsoever. Take your electrolytes – "my yoke is easy and my burden is light" says the Lord" (Matthew 11:30)

Personally, I can't wait to be fit both spiritually and physically. Am I the only one who thinks at times, "Lord, if I was a little lighter I would jump for joy, do somersaults, turn cartwheels and even do the splits for you"? You just don't understand! When I get excited about God, those are things that I would do if I could do them, maybe not in public, but who knows, I may just surprise myself!

Chapter 21

KEEP MOVING TOWARDS THE FINISH LINE

This battle that we are in is also depicted as a race. "Wherefore seeing we also are compassed about with so great a cloud of witnesses, let us lay aside every weight and the sin which doth so easily beset us, and let us run with patience the race that is set before us looking unto Jesus the author and finisher of our faith." (Hebrews 12:1-2)

We are not in this race by ourselves; there are others running in the race with us. The great thing about this race is that it is not about speed. We don't have to worry about not getting a prize because we did not come in first, second or third. In this race, the goal is to make it to the finish line. Most marathons show those who finish first, but sometimes they also show the ones who crossed the finish line many hours later. As human, we don't give much thought to those who come in last, but has made it in spite of the setbacks. Some of these people made it through many adversities, and they crossed the finish line because a special person in their lives were a positive influence, made a huge impact, and have now passed on. Others persevere to prove a point to people who may have said that they couldn't do it. And then there are those who might have had a desire to accomplish that goal before they die. Whatever the reason or however long it took, the important thing was that they made it.

Some marathoners are left behind because of some perceived handicap. Because they are slower than the other runners, they watch people whizz past them; and some of those other runners may feel that the slower runners don't have what it takes to make it. But consider this: they all had to prepare for this day for a long time. Yet even knowing that, some runners give up when they see that they are not going to be first, second or even third.

Don't Give Up

There are even some runners who give up when they get thirsty, hungry, need to use the restroom, got tired and felt like they were too far behind. Let me say to this: please run this race with patience, "looking unto Jesus the author and finisher of our faith". (Hebrews 12:2) When you encounter obstacles, be patient, as this too will pass – "weeping may endure for a night but joy comes in the morning". (Psalms 30:5)

Eyes Front

No man or woman who puts his hand to the plow and is looking back is fit for the kingdom of God". (Luke 9:62)

Don't look back saying any of the following:

- *"If I wasn't a Christian, I would have been married and have kids by now."*

- *"If I wasn't a Christian I would have so much money, live in a big house with lots of cars."*

- *"If I wasn't a Christian I would be going to parties every night, but here I am being a church mouse."*

- *"When I wasn't a Christian, I had lots of money, rich friends and could buy whatever I wanted."*

- *"If I wasn't a Christian and someone disrespected me, I would cuss them out like a dog."*

Don't look back! God never said it would always be peaches and cream, but He did promise that he would supply all our needs according to his riches in glory by Christ Jesus. (Philippians 4:19) He promised that He will never leave us nor forsake us (Deuteronomy 31:6). Jesus also promised that he will not give us more than we can bear. (1 Corinthians 10:13) As a matter of fact, he wants you to cast all your cares upon him because he cares for you. (1 Peter 5:7) Jesus asks you to seek first the kingdom of God and his righteousness and all other things shall be added unto you. (Matthew 6:33) Do I need to go on? I'll borrow a phrase from one of my former pastors who used to say, "If you mind God's business, he will mind yours." So don't worry, God's got you!

We are living in these last days where Christians, even those who have known God for a long time, are throwing in the towel and giving up on God, and for what? Mark 8:36 clearly poses this question: "What shall it profit a man if he should gain the whole world and lose his own soul?" Just think about it. "Who or what shall separate you or me from the love of God? Is it tribulation, distress, persecution, famine, nakedness, peril or sword?" (Romans 8:35- 39)

In 2 Kings 5, Gehazi, Elisha's servant, had seen Elisha work miracles by the hand of the Lord, and was instrumental in Naaman being cured from leprosy. No doubt he was thinking that some monetary compensation was in order. Gehazi saw that Naaman was a wealthy man and he allowed his greed to control him until he lied to Naaman. Naaman gave Gehazi all the things he desired, but ultimately he ended up losing more than he gained, for he also acquired leprosy. Now what good were those fine garments? They were of no use to him because he now had leprosy and was an outcast from society. What did it profit him? Not a thing.

What are you holding onto that is keeping you from where God wants you to go, from walking into your destiny? What or who is so special to you that you are willing to lose your soul over? The songwriter Nancy Harmon sings the song "I've Come Too Far to Look Back". You also have come too far to look back. Lot's wife became a pillar of salt because she looked back. She looked back at the riches, the fame, the popularity, the friends she left behind and the life she held dear, all that she wasn't going to be a part of again. Looking back, she gained nothing, but rather, lost everything – her life.

Fight the good fight of faith, "looking unto Jesus the author and finisher of our faith" (Hebrews 12:2) If you look back, you are losing ground. If you look back, you can't see clearly what is in front of you. If you look back, you will become stiff-necked. If you look back, you most definitely will lose your way.

Keep moving towards the finish line for retreat is not an option. In this life we are given so many choices in practically every area of our daily living. There are choices of what schools to attend, whether online or in a classroom setting, whether to go out-of-state or stay in your community. There are choices on the career you want to pursue, whether to go full-time or part-time, whether to take out student loans or pay out-of-pocket. When it comes to dressing, there also are quite a few choices: whether to be casual, formal or just plain comfortable. Food choices: fast food, home-cooked meals, junk food, to diet or be a vegetarian, to eat whatever you like, or to eat healthy. They are so many choices that at times we make the wrong choice.

When I was growing up we were poor, so I did not have many options in regard to food, clothing, school, church or friends. I was taught to eat what was set before me and ask no questions. I had to either eat it or leave it. Most of the time I had to eat it or wait till the next day to eat, and there was no guarantee that the next meal would be something that I would like. Don't get me wrong, to have options are good, but with options comes the responsibility to make rational and right decisions. Just the other day, my neighbor was complaining about a decision her son made. She said he had a good job that was willing to pay for his college, but he left the job for another that was paying four dollars more. Now that is what's wrong with us sometimes we want a quick fix, instead of us looking at the big picture down the road and what would be in our best interest.

Some of us, after we've made the wrong decision, mess up our lives and waste precious time, end up going back to the starting point, then head in the right direction. This does not need to be you. The word of God clearly states in Proverbs 3: 6 that "in all our ways we should acknowledge him and he will direct our path". Regardless of what may come our way - the obstacles, the pitfalls, the disappointments, the confusion and the frustrations - keep moving toward the finish line. It will all be worth it in the end.

Remember: you cannot do it on your own, you do not have the strength; but God's strength in you is where it's at. His strength will be made perfect in your weakness. (2 Corinthians 12:9)

Chapter 22

SENIORITY DOES NOT NECESSARILLY MEAN SINCERITY

As we are coming to the end of this book, I want to admonish you ever so earnestly to fight the good fight of faith, and to keep moving towards the finish line. In 1 Kings 13, the prophet, who was also called "the man of God" made some terrible mistakes by taking advice from the wrong person. It was an old backslidden prophet who had been in the fight for a long time, but ultimately lost his way. He had lost the anointing but was still pretending to be saved, sanctified and filled with the precious Holy Spirit. Sometimes when a person is older and more seasoned we just assume that they are somehow closer to God than we are, and maybe have a word of wisdom or some prophetic declaration to speak into our lives. That is not always the case.

Some may see the anointing on your life and instead of being happy for you, they are filled with jealousy because it just reminds them of where they used to be with God. They are filled with envy because, instead of finding their way back to God, they gave up and are now making it their goal in life to frustrate your walk with God, giving you false instructions under the pretense of encouragement.

But don't let them.

Try the Spirit

Matthew 7:21 says "not all who say to me Lord, Lord will enter into the kingdom of heaven". If someone is giving you advice that is contrary to the word of the Lord, watch that person, and stay clear of them. It may be that the spirit of the Lord has already left that person. There are examples in the Bible, such as King Saul. King Saul, who had no peace or rest when the spirit of the Lord left him, tried to kill David... and all David was trying to do was calm the King's spirit by playing the harp!

I once asked a spiritual leader what he thought about "trying on the shoes before buying it" in regards to sex before marriage. He informed me that it was okay to know what you are getting before actually sealing the deal. I knew what the Bible said concerning this issue, but I wanted his opinion. And he gave me the wrong advice.

There are times when you feel pressured to do certain things and people would have you believe that you are old-fashioned, too rigid, too much of a holy roller, that you should go with the flow and with the times that we are living in, But I want to tell you that the word of God does not change. Both Matthew 24:35 and Mark 13:31 declare that "heaven and earth shall pass away but my words shall not pass away". It is always right to do the right. "The foundation of God stands sure, having this seal, the Lord knows them that are his, and let everyone that name the name of Christ depart from iniquity." 2 Timothy 2:19

Everyone who calls themselves Christians or even preachers may not adhere or abide by the same standards as you do, or to the words of the Lord. Don't be fooled by their fame, fortune, or influence. The only thing that matters is that they are led by the spirit of the Lord.

Slacken Not Your Riding

In 1 Kings 13, the story is told of a man of God who was travelling from Judah to Bethel. He had an unpleasant message to deliver to the evil king Jeroboam. He delivered the message and even declared that he would be shown a sign. Upon hearing the word of lord brought forth by the man prophet, he stretched forth his hand against the man of god, and immediately his hand shriveled up, and the sign that was spoken of, took place. Now when this happened, the king begged the man of God to pray to have his hand restored, he prayed and it was done. The king wanted to show his gratitude and therefore invited the prophet to dinner and was willing to give him a reward, but the prophet kindly refused because the Lord had told him not to eat or drink there and to return home using a different route than the one that he used to get there.

There were observers and among them were the sons of an old prophet, who relayed to him the events of the day, and to put it in a nutshell, he went after the man of God and found him sitting under an oak tree. He had slackened his riding! He was making himself comfortable in the wrong place. Yes, as humans we get tired and weary of travelling spiritually speaking, but that is the time that we need to hurry up and run home. Run to God who is our source!

The oak tree, like the one the man of God was sitting under, has many branches and leaves that is good for shade, and as I consider this, and as the spirit revealed to me, it could likened to someone who is in authority and has others working under him. Branches, limbs and covering represent those who are in charge of others and the leaves are those who look to him as a source of their everyday livelihood and spiritual edification. Sometimes we put our trust in others more than we do in God, and it is high time that we rectify that.

The man of God was successful in refusing the Kings offer to dine with him, but here he is sitting at ease. He did head in the right direction, but he was supposed to keep it moving. As I said before, "The race is not for the swift, or the battle for the strong, but those that endure to the end the same shall be saved". (Ecclesiastes 9:11)

It is only logical to assume that if I can't eat or drink in the place where I am, that means that I will need to hurry up, and get out of that place, and to try reach my destination as soon as possible. I don't want to sit under a tree, when my nice cozy soft bed is calling my name, and my soothing sofa is waiting for me at home where I can relax and have something to eat and drink. My God, I just preached to the choir.

I am in a place where God wants me to limit my eating and drinking so that he can take me to a place where eating and drinking would not be an issue for me, where I esteem the word of God more than my necessary food as stated by Job in Job 23:12. Yet here I am being slothful, getting fat on the food instead of getting fat on the word of God. God has told some of us that we need to live a life of fasting but have we been obedient? We have to pass this test. We have to deny ourselves eating and drinking temporarily in order to obtain the vast and countless blessings that He has in store for us. Thank you Lord!

Brothers and sisters, our prayer should be identical to Job's "that when he tries me, I shall come forth like pure gold". (Job 23:10) Yes he knows the way that we take, nothing is hid from him. Slacken not your riding in the right direction. The old prophet came to the man of God and said that he was a prophet just like he was and lied and told him that God had told him that he was to come back to his house and eat and drink with him. He listened to him and disobeyed God, and in the end his body was torn to pieces by a loin who knew better than to eat his flesh. (Read the chapter for yourself – I Kings 13.)

It is amazing how animals could obey the voice of the lord, like in the story of Balaam and his donkey in Numbers chapter 22, and even Jonah and the big fish in Jonah chapter 1, and we who are bone of his bone, and flesh of his flesh choose to be disobedient. I admonish you, do not slacken your riding while fighting this good fight of faith.

~~~

Do not slacken your riding

~~~

Chapter 23

LOOK OUT FOR LIARS

Two things mentioned in Proverbs 6:16-19 that God hates is a lying tongue and a false witness that speaks lies.

As I look at these verses I see that the old prophet mentioned in the previous chapter was guilty of all the things that the Lord hates and I could not help but wonder what became of him. As terrible as that prophet may seem, God's grace is of such that if "we confess our sins, he is faithful and just to forgive us of our sins and cleanse us from all unrighteousness". 1 John 1:9

If you are guilty of any of these today, ask God to cleanse you and forgive you so that you would do his will and to be pleasing in his sight. "White lies" are still lies and "bending the truth a little" is also a lie.

Be careful that you don't say "God told me" when it is your own opinion and your intuition. Be aware also of those who say "God told me to tell you", and those who use God to bring profit to themselves. Such as those who say "if you want to know who your enemies are", "if you want to be delivered from witchcraft", just bring in a certain amount of money and I will lay hands on you and tell you what you need to do. Basically, be aware of false prophets who actually are wolves in sheep's clothing.

~~~

Be aware of false prophets

~~~

Chapter 24

WATCH WHO YOU DINE WITH

The Bible clearly states in 1 Corinthians 5:11 that there are those who you should not keep company with. This does not mean that you avoid them altogether; in fact, I would encourage you to pray for them and love them. However, there is a limit to how far you go in your association with those persons. Two very wise sayings about this very thing go like this:

"You are known by the company you keep."

And

"Birds of a feather flock together."

You may say Jesus ate with publicans and sinners. Yes he did, and he made an impact on their lives. The people we are talking about are the ones that have no desire to change their way of living, those who the spirit of the Lord might have left, and who could influence you, instead of you influencing them and leading them down the path of the straight and narrow.

There are people who look at your every move, and who read your life like a book. You don't know everyone who knows you, and you are to live a life that would not cause you to be a stumbling block to anyone.

If you eat pork that it offends your brother, do not eat pork in his presence. Even though you don't have a conviction that eating pork is wrong, nevertheless if you know that it will cause your brother or sister who is weaker to fall, you must refrain from eating it in their presence. This is just one example because if you're eating it in faith, it is blessed of God.

Some may say "I don't care what he or she thinks" or "I'll eat or drink what I want"; but that should not be the case for the Bible says "as far as possible, live peaceably with all men". (Romans 12:18)

Bread and water are basic nourishment, and sometimes we have to put these aside. We often take basic things for granted and don't realize how important they are until they are taken away from us. Let us appreciate all that God bestows upon us, and never feel that anything is too much or too valuable to give up if God tells us so. Trust me; he has something better for you down the road if you will be obedient. Isaiah 1:19-20 warns us that" only the willing and the obedient shall eat the good of the land, but they that refuse and rebel shall be devoured by the sword". I don't know about you, but I don't want anything or anyone, let alone a full belly, to keep me from all that God has for me!

Chapter 25

KEEP YOUR ROBES UNSPOTTED

In this fight, we are given the full armor of God, but under that armor we should be wearing our rules of righteousness. This rule was given to us when Jesus shed his blood on the cross of Calvary for our sins. He paid the ultimate price so that you and I could live and have life more abundantly. By his blood that was shed we are made right and we have righteousness - not on our own, but through <u>his</u> righteousness. By accepting the shed blood of Christ we have become justified as if we'd never sinned. Revelation 19:80

This robe of righteousness is white, and you know how easily white gets dirty and stained. However, we are to maintain our white robes by going to the Crimson Stream Laundromat of God's blood for our daily cleansing. We need that cleansing hourly, every minute, and every second. One songwriter put it this way: "I need thee, oh I need thee, every hour I need thee. Oh bless me now my savior, I come to thee."

We have to keep our robes unspotted in order to make it to the marriage supper of the Lamb. This is warfare and we have to be always on guard, on the lookout, and vigilant. There is no time to relax and be at ease. Amos 6:1 reads thus: "Woe to those who are at ease in Zion". When we relax, we get comfortable, and when we get comfortable, we might want to sit down or even lay down. Before we know it, we're sleeping! There is no time for spiritual sleep. Anything can happen when we fall asleep so we must stand strong, keep our eyes open and focused on Jesus with our feet firmly planted on the word of God.

This is a little song that God gave me some years ago as I was preparing to teach a Bible study class.

Keep your robes unspotted
Keep your garments pure and white
Keep your robes unspotted for the marriage of the Lamb is nigh.

Keep fighting the good fight of faith!

God bless you.

ABOUT THE AUTHOR

 Lois Kirwan is a certified surgical technologist, a licensed and ordained minister, and has a Bachelor's degree in Communications. After the death of her mother, Lois migrated to the United States from the very small island of Montserrat at the tender age of 19 in search of a better life. She did various odd jobs to take care of her kids while putting herself through college.

Because of her unrelenting faith in God, Evangelist Lois Kirwan is able to share her struggles through depression, rape, low self-esteem, domestic abuse, and even bigamy. As a single parent, Evangelist Lois also shares how God supplies her needs and is everything that she needs Him to be. She states, "If He could do it for me, He could do the same for you."

Through her many talents as a writer, song writer, singer and comedian, Evangelist Lois dedicates her life to sharing the love of God to many near and far, and to win the lost at any cost.

.